Madagascar Wildlife

A VISITOR'S GUIDE

Nick Garbutt
Daniel Austin
with
Derek Schuurman

edition
4

www.bradtguides.com

Bradt Travel Guides Ltd, UK
The Globe Pequot Press Inc, USA

Reprinted February 2017
Fourth Edition published November 2014
First published 1996

Bradt Travel Guides Ltd
IDC House, The Vale, Chalfont St Peter, Bucks SL9 9RZ, England
www.bradtguides.com
Published in the USA by The Globe Pequot Press Inc,
PO Box 480, Guilford, Connecticut 06437-0480

British Library Cataloguing in Publication Data
A catalogue record for this book is available from the British Library

ISBN-13: 978 1 84162 557 7
e-ISBN: 978 1 78477 106 5 (epub)
e-ISBN: 978 1 78477 206 2 (mobi)

Photographs
Franco Andreone (FA), Daniel Austin (DA), Len de Beer (LdB), Paul Bertner (PB)
Jim Bond (JB), Hilary Bradt (HB), Marius Burger (MB),
Callan Cohen/Birding Africa (CC/BA), Paul Cornish (PC), Adrian Deneys (AD),
Devin Edmonds (DE), Brian L Fisher (BF), Karen Freeman (KF),
Nick Garbutt/Indri Images (NG), Nick Garbutt/NaturePL (NG/NPL),
Nick Garbutt/NHPA (NG/NHPA), Moritz Grubemann (MG), Louise Jasper (LJ),
Bill Love (BL), Kyle Lussier (KL), Ioannis Magouras (IM), Pete Oxford (PO),
Colin Radford (CR), David Rogers (DR), John Roff (JR), Patrick Schönecker (PS),
Harald Schütz (HS), Derek Schuurman (DS), Joe Tobias (JT),
Mike Wilson (MW), Ariadne Van Zandbergen (AVZ)

Front cover Male panther chameleon (NG)
Back cover Verreaux's sifaka (NG)
Title page (from top to bottom):
Helmet vanga (NG), ring-tailed lemur (CR), Madagascar giant day gecko (DA)
Contents page ring-tailed lemur (NG/NPL)

Map David McCutcheon FBCart.S

Designed and formatted by Pepenbury Ltd
Production managed by Jellyfish Print Solutions; printed in India

CONTENTS

Box features

ACKNOWLEDGEMENTS

The authors would like to thank the following for their advice, information and assistance: Franco Andreone, Hery Andrianiantefana, Olivier Behra, Jim Bond, Corinna Botoulas, Marius Burger, Rainer Dolch, Lee Durrell, Devin Edmonds, Frank Glaw, Caroline Harcourt, Clare Hargreaves, Hilton Hastings, Frank Hawkins, Mike and Liz Howe, Richard Jenkins, Alison Jolly, Olivier Langrand, David Lees, Richard Lewis, Russ Mittermeier, Maya Moore, Mike Picker, Gilbert Rakotarisoa, Nivo Ravelojaona, Don Reid, Gerold Schipper, Harald Schütz, Natalie Seddon, Ian Sinclair, Hilana Steyn, Miguel Vences, Lucienne Wilmé and Pat Wright.

Several photographers kindly allowed us to use their images free of charge. Without their generosity this book could not have been so fully illustrated. In this regard we are indebted to: Franco Andreone, Len de Beer, Paul Bertner, Jim Bond, Hilary Bradt, Marius Burger, Callan Cohen, Paul Cornish, Adrian Deneys, Devin Edmonds, Brian L Fisher, Karen Freeman, Moritz Grubemann, Louise Jasper, Bill Love, Kyle Lussier, Ioannis Magouras, Colin Radford, John Roff, David Rogers, Patrick Schönecker, Derek Schuurman, Joe Tobias, Mike Wilson and Ariadne Van Zandbergen.

Twig-mimic snake (see page 173) (HB)

ABOUT THE AUTHORS

Nick Garbutt (*www.nickgarbutt.com*) is a well-known authority on Madagascar's wildlife. He first visited the island in 1991, backpacking for a month and visiting four parks. He has returned every year since and in doing so has travelled the length and breadth of the island, repeatedly visiting all the major national parks and reserves, as well as many remote regions. He has seen the majority of the island's lemurs and other mammals in the wild, as well as a very high proportion of the other endemic fauna – a claim few can make.

He is the principal photographer in this book and his awards include two category wins in the *Wildlife Photographer of the Year* competition. Nick's passion for Madagascar remains undiminished and he continues to lead photographic tours each year. He is also author of *Mammals of Madagascar: A Complete Guide*, *Chameleons*, *Wild Borneo* and Bradt's *100 Animals to See Before They Die*, as well as a regular contributor of articles and images to publications including *National Geographic*, *Terra Mater*, *BBC Wildlife*, *Africa Geographic* and *Wild Travel*.

Daniel Austin is a naturalist, photographer and researcher of all things Malagasy. His fascination with this extraordinary country extends from its flora and fauna to its people and their culture, with a particular interest in the island's frogs and reptiles. He is also co-author of both the award-winning Bradt *Madagascar* guidebook and the *Madagascar Highlights* guide. As well as in these books, his photographs have appeared in various media including scientific publications, travel magazines, and charity calendars.

Daniel also occasionally lectures on and accompanies tours to the island, in between researching new editions of the guidebooks. He is secretary of the Anglo-Malagasy Society (*www.anglo-malagasysociety.co.uk*), which holds regular events in London to raise the profile of Madagascar in the UK, and he also maintains an extensive library of books, maps and other documents on all aspects of the country (*www.madagascar-library.com*).

CONTRIBUTORS

The authors are especially grateful to **Derek Schuurman** for his assistance with this edition. A keen naturalist, Derek works at Rainbow Tours and has well over two decades' experience in the travel industry as a Madagascar specialist. He co-authors the Globetrotter *Madagascar Travel Guide* and has contributed to many other books and articles on Madagascar.

Earlier editions of this book have benefited from the input of other expert contributors. **Hilary Bradt** (*www.hilarybradt.com*), founder of Bradt Travel Guides, first visited Madagascar in 1976, started leading tours there in 1982, and published the first guidebook to the country in 1984. **John Roff** is a naturalist and environmental educator, qualified by over 35 years of ongoing research, exploration and field experience, with a special interest in spiders and insects. **Len de Beer** is a ninth-generation South African who has lived and taught in Namibia, Kenya, South Korea and Madagascar. He has a BSc (Hons) in Entomology and delights in sharing the marvels of the insect world with young minds.

Aye-aye (see page 82) (NG)

AN INTRODUCTION TO THE WILDLIFE OF MADAGASCAR

Of Madagascar I can say to naturalists that it is truly their promised land. There Nature seems to have retreated into a private sanctuary to work on models other than those she has created elsewhere. At every step one encounters the most strange and marvellous forms.

Joseph Philibert Commerson, 1771

Madagascar had been enchanting naturalists long before Charles Darwin visited the Galápagos and began developing his theories on evolution. Unlike these islands, which were born through volcanic eruptions, Madagascar was once part of a huge supercontinent that covered most of the southern hemisphere. Some 200 million years ago (mya), when dinosaurs dominated the earth (the oldest dinosaur fossils ever discovered are from southern Madagascar and date back 230 million years), Gondwana began to break up and the present-day continents of Africa, South America, India, Antarctica and Australia slowly separated.

Madagascar (with India still attached) broke free from Africa some 165mya and drifted southeastward. The island had reached its current position by 80mya, when the Indian portion became detached, leaving Madagascar isolated along with all its stowaway dinosaurs. However, strong links between present-day reptiles in Madagascar and South America, suggest that land bridges probably once connected the two via Antarctica.

Nonetheless, the majority of the more recently evolved life forms we see today arrived after Madagascar had become isolated. Most likely, the ancestors of land mammals – and many of the reptiles and even frogs – rafted across the Mozambique Channel on floating clumps of vegetation washed out to sea after heavy storms. Few survived this perilous crossing, and consequently many of Africa's familiar groups are absent from Madagascar: the cats and dogs, along with their prey animals, antelopes and other ungulates.

Geological forces thrust up the high mountain range that runs down the centre of the island, creating dramatically different climates: wet in the east, dry in the west and drier still in the south. The flora developed according to this distribution of rainfall and the fauna subsequently evolved to occupy the many niches on the new mini-continent: rainforest, deciduous forest, mountains and semi-desert. No-one can say how many species there are today in Madagascar – perhaps more than 200,000 – but it is known that the majority are found nowhere else. Over 80% of the wildlife is unique to the island (endemic) and much of it is startlingly different from anything found elsewhere in the world.

1

The subfossil skull of an extinct giant lemur, excavated from a limestone cave at Anjajavy (NG)

Two to three thousand years ago an all-conquering predator arrived in this Eden: man. Within just one thousand years, some 25 large animals had been wiped out, including at least 17 species of lemur (some as large as gorillas), three pygmy hippos and the largest bird that ever lived, the elephant bird (*Aepyornis maximus*). Another thousand years passed before man recognised his folly and started protecting instead of destroying. In 1927 the French colonial government created the first reserves. But conservation took a back seat after independence in 1960 until international interest in this natural treasure trove prompted the Malagasy government to instigate a conservation programme in the mid-1980s.

Today, Madagascar is considered one of the world's top conservation priorities. Since 2003 the area of protected forests has been tripled and new national parks and reserves have been created, involving local people in the decision-making. Ecotourism offers the nation's best chance of earning the foreign currency needed to continue its efforts to save its priceless natural heritage.

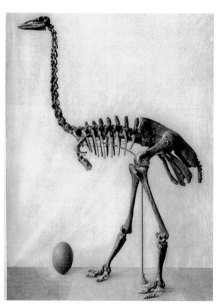

Skeleton of an elephant bird from *Paléontologie de Madagascar* by Monnier (1913) shown alongside a man for scale. This huge flightless bird is probably the largest that ever lived. It is believed to have become extinct only relatively recently, around the time of the dodo. Subfossil eggshells and even complete eggs can still be found in the south of Madagascar.

EVOLUTION

Why is the wildlife of Madagascar so different? To find the answer, we need to understand the forces that create all living things: the forces of evolution.

Individuals of a species differ slightly from one another; these differences are the result of variations in their genetic make-up. Sometimes these differences convey an advantage that gives the individual a better chance of survival; that is to say improves its 'fitness'. It follows that such individuals are more likely to breed successfully and, crucially, pass the beneficial genes to their offspring. This is called **natural selection**. With successive generations advantageous genes become more prevalent in the population.

Organisms live in constantly changing environments, and individuals with characteristics that best suit the prevailing conditions will survive at the expense of those that are less well suited. Over successive generations these favourable characteristics (adaptations) will accumulate by natural selection and gradually cause the organism to alter. This is **evolution**.

When Madagascar became isolated, conditions on the new island were different from those on the neighbouring continents. With time, the founding stock of animals and plants evolved in response to their new circumstances, to become new species – a process called **speciation**. And because Madagascar was isolated there were no diluting influences from the mainland, so the new species could develop in singular and unique ways.

However, some species in Madagascar do show some similarities to species in other parts of the world. For example, the Malagasy mantella frogs look and behave very much like the poison dart frogs from Central and South America, even though they are only distantly related. Both live similar lifestyles under similar conditions, so natural selection has independently arrived at the same solution: this is known as **convergent evolution**.

The green-backed (climbing) mantella (*Mantella laevigata*) from Madagascar (*far left* DA) shows striking similarity to this unrelated poison dart frog from South America (*left* NG) – an example of convergent evolution.

This may also happen to unrelated organisms living in the same area, where they develop common characteristics (through convergent evolution) and then continue to evolve along similar lines, so that their resemblances become quite striking – a process called **parallel evolution**. For example, the true sunbirds (family Nectariniidae) and sunbird-asities (family Philepittidae) in Madagascar.

TECHNICAL TERMS

We have tried to make this book accessible to everyone, but the use of some technical terms is unavoidable. Here are some you will encounter.

Nocturnal	Active only under cover of darkness (at night).
Diurnal	Active only during daylight hours.
Cathemeral	Active both by day and by night.
Crepuscular	Active only during the twilight hours around dawn and dusk.
Larva	The immature stage in an insect's life cycle between the egg and the pupa, such as a caterpillar or maggot. The pupa then undergoes complete metamorphosis into a mature adult.
Nymph	The immature stage of an insect that resembles the adult form and develops in gradual steps (eg: crickets and grasshoppers).
Hibernation	A state of inactivity resembling deep sleep in which an animal lowers its metabolic rate in response to cold (normally winter) and survives on fat reserves laid down during the summer.
Aestivation	A state of inactivity similar to hibernation, but in response to a dry period (normally summer) rather than cold.
Endemic	Restricted to a particular geographic region, often due to isolation, as with islands. For example, crowned lemurs as a species are endemic to northern Madagascar, while their family (Lemuridae) is endemic to the island as a whole.
Indigenous	Originating and occurring naturally in a particular region; native.
Exotic	Introduced from elsewhere, either deliberately or accidentally to a region to which the species is not indigenous.
Niche	The role of an organism within its environment and with respect to the communities of other organisms that share its environment.

CLASSIFICATION

Biologists have created a strict set of rules to identify organisms precisely. This is called **classification** or **taxonomy** and an understanding of its principles will help clarify the descriptions in this book.

The first division, called a kingdom, is very broadly defined, for instance animal, plant or fungus. Each subsequent division is progressively more precisely defined until the organism is identified as a species. Here are two simplified examples from Madagascar.

Common name:	**Common brown lemur**	**Parson's chameleon**
Kingdom:	Animalia	Animalia
Phylum:	Chordata	Chordata
Class:	Mammalia	Reptilia
Order:	Primates	Squamata
Family:	Lemuridae	Chamaeleonidae
Subfamily:	Lemurinae	Chamaeleoninae
Genus:	*Eulemur*	*Calumma*
Species:	*fulvus*	*parsonii*

4

The chapters in this book broadly correspond to classes of animals: mammals (Mammalia), birds (Aves), reptiles (Reptilia) and frogs (Anura). A species can be referred to by quoting just its genus (plural: genera) and species. Together these constitute the **scientific name**, which is written in italics with the genus capitalised. If the genus is known, but not the species, it is written thus: *Eulemur* sp; or if the description includes several species from the same genus it is written as: *Eulemur* spp.

Some species are further divided into subspecies or races. Often these groups have been separated for relatively short periods, perhaps by geographical barriers like rivers, and evolution has led to differences between the two groups arising, such as in their colour (although they could interbreed to produce hybrids were the populations to regroup). The subspecies name is written after the species name.

RECENT CHANGES IN CLASSIFICATION

The blossoming of research in Madagascar over the past 20 years has resulted in many new species being described. In addition, research has prompted some major changes in the way groups of organisms are thought to relate to one another. Consequently, there have been some significant alterations to the taxonomy of many groups. This is especially true of several lemur families, as well as the Malagasy carnivores (see page 84) some bird families and many reptiles and frogs. The changes in lemur classification warrant explanation.

The majority of lemurs previously considered subspecies have been elevated to full species status. For instance, this means that all the of brown lemurs and sifakas previously described as subspecies are now regarded as distinct species in their own right.

Furthermore, some groups have seen massive explosions in the number of species they contain. This particularly applies to the sportive lemurs (genus *Lepilemur*) and mouse lemurs (genus *Microcebus*). The 1990 *IUCN Red Data Book*: *Lemurs of Madagascar* listed seven species of the former and two of the latter. The list currently recognised by Conservation International stands at 21 mouse lemur species and 26 sportive lemurs. However, most of these were not hitherto-undiscovered forms that had suddenly been found in unexplored corners of the island; rather, the majority represented known populations being reclassified and renamed after the application of modern DNA analysis. Effectively populations once assumed to belong to a certain species have been split off and described as new ones. Some scientists (the 'splitters') use these methods to identify subtle genetic differences between separate populations of a known species. If there are enough differences, they then designate the splinter population as a new species. In the other corner are the 'lumpers' – scientists who do not consider such subtlety as a sufficient basis for distinguishing species. They prefer to base their descriptions on more established and tangible criteria such as anatomical features and behaviour, accepting that there is simply genetic variation inherent across any population. Unsurprisingly, there is a heated debate between the 'splitters' and the 'lumpers'. Ultimately there is no right or wrong answer, which serves to emphasise that it is impossible to define the concept of a species in the first place (there are more that 60 attempts at a definition in the scientific literature).

CONSERVATION – WHAT YOU CAN DO

The years between 2002 and 2009 were good ones for conservation in Madagascar. The government made proactive commitments to ensuring that the country be recognised as a regional leader in ecotourism and the president initiated an increase in protected areas from 1.7 million to 6 million hectares.

Sadly, a coup in 2009 halted much of the progress in its tracks and the international aid money on which many projects depend slowed to a mere trickle. Illegal loggers in particular took advantage of the power vacuum to strip several protected areas of millions of precious rosewood and ebony trees for export to China. Only in 2014 did democratic rule return to the country, but efforts are already under way to renegotiate funding deals and set the conservation wheels in motion once more.

There are now many private, community-run conservation initiatives across the country (Anja is a fine example; see page 42). Guiding associations also continue to be formed at many parks. And several nurseries propagate saplings of endemic trees to create corridors linking isolated forest blocks or rehabilitate severely degraded countryside.

For conservation to succeed, local communities must be partners and beneficiaries in the process. Ecotourism plays an important role too; when responsibly managed, locals benefit and receive incentives to preserve their ecosystems.

Simply by visiting sites profiled in this book you are making a contribution to conservation. Here are a few ideas to make your visit even more beneficial:

- The pioneering ACSAM Initiative (*www.sahonagasy.org*) runs a citizen science project to collate sightings and photos of amphibians in Madagascar.
- BirdLife International's Malagasy partner ASITY conducts important bird conservation work. BirdLife always appreciates donations.
- What better way of literally 'putting something back' than planting an endemic tree? This gratifying experience is offered at Mitsinjo's portion of Analamazaotra Forest and Vohimana (see page 19), Anjozorobe (page 17), Anjajavy (page 29), Macolline (Antalaha), Vohibola (Pangalanes Canal) and Marovasa-Be (northeast of Mahajanga).
- Keen scuba divers can volunteer for a marine conservation expedition with ReefDoctor (*www.reefdoctor.org*) or Blue Ventures (*www.blueventures.org*).
- Avoid buying shells as souvenirs; this trade is causing several populations of endangered marine molluscs to crash.
- In dry regions (southwest especially), keep your water usage to a minimum.
- Try to use hotels and tour operators involved in community development projects. Some are members of the International Ecotourism Society (*www.ecotourism.org*).
- For help organising fieldwork in Madagascar or to find out about projects you can get involved with, contact the Institute for the Conservation of Tropical Environments (*www.ictetropics.org*).

HABITATS AND
WILDLIFE HOTSPOTS

Lac Vert, Andasibe-Mantadia National Park (NG)

Madagascar has a remarkable diversity of habitats and associated flora. With an area of over 587,000km² it is the world's fourth largest island (after Greenland, New Guinea and Borneo), yet its environmental diversity – encompassing rainforest, deciduous forest, arid thorn thicket, high-altitude moorland and wetlands – equals that of an entire continent. This variety has fostered an equivalent diversity of flora and fauna that is unusual enough to rival that of any similar-sized area on earth.

Habitat variety results from climatic variability. Madagascar lies mostly within the tropics and has a corresponding climate. From north to south it spans some 1,510km, between the latitudes 12° and 25° South, and there is notable variation in typical sea-level temperatures: in the far north the annual average is 27°C, dropping to 22°C at the southern extremity.

A backbone of ancient rocks runs from north to south, forming the high plateau. To the east there is an abrupt escarpment, while in the west the highlands slope gently down to the Mozambique Channel. The trade winds bring the prevailing weather from the Indian Ocean; moisture-laden air is forced to rise over the escarpment and consequently drops most of its rain in the east. Western regions lie in a permanent rain shadow, so conditions gradually become hotter and drier towards the west coast. During the summer, a monsoon regime influences the west. This originates in the north, its influence dwindling towards the south. The result is a double rainfall gradient over the island – declining both east to west and north to south – leading to the northeast being the country's wettest region and the southwest the driest.

MADAGASCAR NATIONAL PARKS

Madagascar's national parks and special reserves are administered by Madagascar National Parks (MNP, formerly known as ANGAP). In January 2006 a new management framework was introduced – the System of Protected Areas of Madagascar (SAPM) – to facilitate the creation of new parks and allow for limited exploitation of their natural resources. SAPM aims to:

- safeguard Madagascar's ecosystems;
- promote and conduct research into the potential of Madagascar's biodiversity;
- develop environmental education programs for local people;
- promote commercial applications of the biodiversity, including ecotourism;
- support sustainable development activities adjacent to protected areas.

To enable those living near protected areas to benefit from their conservation, all visitors must purchase an entrance permit, 50% of the revenue from which goes to local communities. Visitors are also required to enlist the services of a local guide (who are usually found at the park office). Guides are trained by MNP, becoming skilled in interpreting and passing on their knowledge of Madagascar's biodiversity. MNP also works with Malagasy and foreign scientists and conservation agencies.

Lowland rainforest at Masoala National Park (NG)

RAINFOREST

Tropical rainforests the world over harbour a greater diversity of life than any other terrestrial habitat. The eastern rainforests of Madagascar are no exception and are home to a biodiversity that is unmatched on the island. This amazing spectrum of life makes the rainforest a living laboratory of experimentation and so it is widely regarded as the most exciting habitat by professional and amateur naturalists alike.

To travellers, most of whom are more familiar with the woodlands of temperate regions dominated by just one or two species (eg: oak and hazel, beech and maple), the scale and variety of trees and plants in a small area of a tropical rainforest is bewildering. This is especially so in Madagascar where the apparent level of diversity is growing constantly with the continual discovery of new species.

The rainforests of Madagascar have different characteristics depending on altitude and rainfall. Subtle local variations mean there are always exceptions to general rules, but most of the protected areas described in this book fall into one of the two categories below.

Lowland rainforest lies below 800m altitude and is drenched with an average 3,500mm of rain per year, with the wettest area (Masoala peninsula) receiving almost 6,000mm! It is similar to tropical rainforests elsewhere, with large trees supported by buttress roots, smaller trees with stilt-like aerial roots, saplings, lianas, epiphytes and ferns. Compared with rainforests of other continents, however, the trees are closer together, the canopy is lower (typically 30–5m), and there are fewer tall trees poking their crowns above the rest. Epiphytic plants such as orchids are abundant and species of *Impatiens* are common.

Mid-altitude montane rainforest is typical of key reserves like Andasibe-Mantadia, Ranomafana and Montagne d'Ambre. It is found from 800m to about 1,400m, above which it is called high-altitude montane forest. Tree ferns are a typical feature and bamboos are common, as are species of *Kalanchoe*. Compared with lowland rainforest, the canopy is lower (average 20–5m), leaves are smaller and tougher, mosses and epiphytes are more abundant, and shrubby undergrowth flourishes as more light reaches the forest floor.

Most of Madagascar's remaining rainforests are concentrated in a band extending from around Iharana (Vohemar) in the north to near Taolagnaro (Fort Dauphin) in the south. Once continuous, this tract of forest has been severely fragmented by the timber industry and – more significantly – through slash-and-burn agriculture.

Other isolated tracts of montane forest occur towards the island's northern tip around Montagne d'Ambre. An area of seasonally moist forest in the northwest, the Sambirano, constitutes a transition between eastern rainforests and western deciduous forests. The main block is centred on Manongarivo and part of the Tsarantanana Massif, but it also extends to the coast and includes the forest remnants on Nosy Be.

Visiting rainforests can be infuriating, as many animals (especially mammals and birds) are not always easy to find. However, several parks and reserves across the country are now easily accessible and some of the wildlife, particularly lemurs, is starting to become habituated. Visits to three or four of these areas would offer ample wildlife-watching opportunities to see a wide cross-section of species.

Paths near to the Petite Cascade at Montagne d'Ambre are particularly good for seeing the ring-tailed vontsira and blue-nosed Boettger's chameleons. (AVZ)

MONTAGNE D'AMBRE (AMBER MOUNTAIN) NATIONAL PARK

Montagne d'Ambre derives its name from the resin that oozes from trees like the *ramy* (*Canarium madagascariense*) and *rotra* (*Eugenia rotra*), a few of which reach 40m. Created in 1958, this was Madagascar's first national park. It is a green oasis in an otherwise parched landscape: Antsiranana (Diego Suarez), less than 30km to the north, receives only 900mm annual rainfall, yet the park is drenched with 3,500mm. This particularly rewarding and beautiful reserve is easy to get to and has a good trail system with labelled trees and points of interest. Lemurs are usually seen and reptiles are abundant, including a wonderful array of chameleons.

Sanford's brown lemur, male (see page 70). Montagne d'Ambre is the easiest place to see this species. (DA)

Habitat and Terrain

An isolated patch of montane rainforest covering an area of 18,200ha between 850m and 1,475m elevation. The park is notable for its bird's nest ferns, tree ferns, orchids, mosses and lianas. Two waterfalls – the Grande Cascade and Petite Cascade – form focal points, and there are crater lakes (Lac de la Coupe Verte and La Grande Lac) and viewpoints over the forest and surrounding area.

Key Species
MAMMALS

Sanford's brown lemur, crowned lemur, Ankarana sportive lemur, Amber Mountain fork-marked lemur, northern rufous mouse lemur and northern ring-tailed vontsira (*Galidia elegans dambrensis*). Also occasionally sighted is the rare eastern falanouc (*Eupleres goudotii*) – but the latest evidence suggests the western falanouc (*Eupleres major*) occurs there as well.

BIRDS

Madagascar crested ibis, Madagascar malachite kingfisher, Amber Mountain rock-thrush, Madagascar magpie-robin, Madagascar cuckoo-roller, pitta-like ground-roller, Madagascar paradise flycatcher, Madagascar white-throated rail and hook-billed vanga.

Impatiens tuberosa (DA)

REPTILES

Madagascar tree boa (*Sanzinia madagascariensis*), Amber Mountain chameleon (*Calumma ambreense*), Boettger's chameleon (*C. boettgeri*), panther chameleon (*Furcifer pardalis*), leaf-tailed geckos (*Uroplatus sikorae*, *U. ebenaui*, *U. alluaudi* and *U. giganteus*), several stump-tailed chameleons (*Brookesia tuberculata*, *B. ebenaui*, *B. stumpffi* and *B. ambreensis*) and day geckos including the Madagascar giant day gecko (*Phelsuma grandis*).

Visitor Information

Day trips from Antsiranana are possible, but it is better to stay in the vicinity (three reasonable lodges are to be found at nearby Joffreville). There are many easy trails, the areas around which are good for mammals, birds and reptiles. Nocturnal walks are not permitted in the park itself, but one of the lodges – Domaine de Fontenay – manages a 300ha private reserve where night walks are rewarding. The wildlife at Fontenay Nature Park is broadly similar to that of the national park, albeit less diverse.

The Marojejy Massif (HB)

MAROJEJY NATIONAL PARK

Marojejy lies towards the northern extreme of the rainforest band and comprises some of its most remote and unexplored areas. The relative inaccessibility is in part due to the ruggedness of this mountainous massif. The area's flora and fauna are extremely rich and diverse. Virtually all endemic rainforest bird species have been recorded around Marojejy; no fewer than ten lemur species are known from the area; and there are countless reptiles and frogs, many new to science. The area became a national park in 1998.

Habitat and Terrain

The broad variation in altitude (75–2,132m) results in considerable habitat diversity, from dense lowland rainforests, where the canopy exceeds 30m, to high-altitude cloud forest, moist montane scrub and even ericoid thickets close to the peaks. The terrain is demanding and gradients are often very steep. Annual rainfall exceeds 4,000mm and there is no dry season of note.

Key Species

MAMMALS

Silky sifaka, white-fronted brown lemur, red-bellied lemur, northern grey bamboo lemur, eastern woolly lemur, greater dwarf lemur, Seal's sportive lemur, hairy-eared dwarf lemur, mouse lemur, aye-aye, spotted fanaloka (*Fossa fossana*), fosa (*Cryptoprocta ferox*), eastern ring-tailed vontsira (*Galidia elegans elegans*), eastern red forest rat, lowland streaked tenrec and eastern sucker-footed bat.

BIRDS

Helmet vanga, hook-billed vanga, velvet asity, common sunbird-asity, yellow-bellied sunbird-asity, short-legged ground-roller, scaly ground-roller, rufous-headed ground-roller, blue coua, red-fronted coua, red-breasted coua and Madagascar cuckoo-roller.

REPTILES AND FROGS

Leaf-tailed geckos (*Uroplatus giganteus*, *U. ebenaui*, *U. sikorae* and *U. lineatus*), short-horned chameleon (*Calumma brevicorne*), Boettger's chameleon, stump-tailed chameleons (*Brookesia* spp), Madagascar tree boa, and a myriad of frogs including three mantellas (*Mantella laevigata*, *M. manery* and *M. nigricans*).

Visitor Information

Marojejy lies directly to the north of Andapa, 70km inland from the coastal town of Sambava. Access is via the village of Manantenina on the Sambava-to-Andapa road. From Manantenina the park boundary is around two hours on foot. The first camp (Camp Mantella, 450m) is a further two-hour walk from the park boundary, and the second camp (Camp Marojejia, 750m) is an hour beyond that. Both have huts with bunks and flush toilets. The third camp (Camp Simpona, 1,250m) is three hours' hike past Camp Marojejia. A visit of three to five days is recommended. Areas around Camp Mantella are best for helmet vangas, while silky sifakas can be found

The red ruffed lemur (see page 71) is restricted to Masoala. (NG)

in the forests above Camp Marojejia. Walking, particularly at higher elevations, is tough and the hike to the summit is very strenuous. Guides, porters and minor provisions can be arranged through the park office in Manantenina (see *www.marojejy.com*).

Those with spare time may like to call in at Antanetiambo Nature Reserve, 6km from Andapa. This 14ha forested hill was established as a protected area thanks to a self-taught and award-winning environmentalist and accomplished local guide named Desiré Rabary. This small but inspiring reserve is active in local conservation education (with emphasis on sustainable development) and social and environmental improvement projects including fish farming and reforestation. Among the wildlife present are habituated northern bamboo lemurs (*Hapalemur occidentalis*).

MASOALA NATIONAL PARK AND SURROUNDS

The Masoala peninsula has the largest remaining area of lowland rainforest in Madagascar, which extends right down to the shore in places. The total area of the peninsula exceeds 400,000ha with the park occupying some 230,000ha of largely primary forest on the western side. Masoala has arguably the greatest biodiversity in all of Madagascar and efforts to conserve it against the encroachment of agriculture and logging are of vital importance. Fortunately several conservation bodies are active in the region. The national park also includes three marine reserves.

Running northwest of Masoala and continuing all the way up to Marojejy, a vast 372,470ha low- and mid-altitude reserve called Makira Natural Park was established in 2012. So far it has only the most rudimentary infrastructure for tourism. Unfortunately Makira and neighbouring areas have been heavily plundered by illegal bushmeat hunting and loggers extracting endemic rosewood and ebony, to the extent that the Atsinanana Rainforests (collectively including Masoala, Marojejy and some other forests further south) have been included in UNESCO's list of World Heritage Sites in Danger since 2010.

Habitat and Terrain
The canopy height is around 30m and there are few emergent trees. The understorey is characterised by abundant palms, tree ferns and numerous epiphytes and orchids. The slopes are often very steep, with many clear, fast-flowing streams and small rivers. This is the wettest part of Madagascar; annual rainfall averages 5,000–6,000mm and there is no distinct dry season.

Key Species
MAMMALS
Red ruffed lemur (locally endemic), white-fronted brown lemur, Masoala woolly lemur, eastern fork-marked lemur, aye-aye, mouse lemur, spotted fanaloka, eastern falanouc, eastern ring-tailed vontsira, lowland red forest rat, greater hedgehog tenrec and lowland streaked tenrec.

BIRDS
Much sought after, but very difficult to see, are the Madagascar serpent eagle, Madagascar red owl and Bernier's vanga. Regularly seen are the helmet vanga, nuthatch vanga, red-breasted coua, scaly ground-roller, short-legged ground-roller, Madagascar wood rail and velvet asity.

REPTILES AND FROGS
Various chameleons including panther chameleon, Boettger's chameleon, stump-tailed chameleons (*Brookesia* spp), leaf-tailed geckos (*Uroplatus fimbriatus* and *U. lineatus*), day geckos (*Phelsuma* spp), tomato frog (*Dyscophus antongilii*), *Mantella ebenaui* and green-backed (climbing) mantella (*M. laevigata*).

Visitor Information
The peninsula lies to the east of Maroantsetra and forms the eastern coastline of Antongil Bay. It is accessible most easily by boat, 1½–3hrs from Maroantsetra. The best areas of forest (especially for red ruffed lemurs) are near Lohatrozona and Andranobe, while the secondary coastal forest at Tampolo can be good for birding. There are at least six lodges of varying standard. The main forest areas have good trail systems, which are difficult and steep in parts. Potentially wet throughout the year, but dry spells are possible anytime. The best months to visit are September to December. A visit of at least three days is recommended for this wonderful area.

Also in the vicinity are the island special reserve of Nosy Mangabe (see the following section) and Fanankaraina Forest Tropical Park. Co-managed by locals and an international group of zoological gardens, Fanankaraina is a 1,650ha protected area situated a 9km boat ride east of Maroantsetra. It is regarded as one

Being usually solitary, it is rare to see two aye-ayes together (see page 82). (PC)

of the best places in Madagascar to seek wild aye-ayes year-round, and is also excellent for the white-browed owl (*Ninox superciliaris*) and Glen's long-fingered bat (*Miniopterus gleni*).

NOSY MANGABE SPECIAL RESERVE

An island in Antongil Bay, Nosy Mangabe has been a popular centre for research since 1966 when several aye-ayes were released there. Groups of black-and-white ruffed lemurs and white-fronted brown lemurs were also introduced prior to this and are thriving.

Habitat and Terrain

Lowland rainforest (similar to Masoala) covers the 520ha island. This has largely regenerated after considerable logging over two centuries ago. There are large buttress-rooted trees reaching over 35m in height. Species typical of this type of forest include: *Ravensara, Canarium, Ocotea, Ficus* and *Tambourissa*. Tree ferns, ferns, epiphytes and orchids are also common. The island's slopes rise steeply from the sea to the summit at 331m.

Key Species
MAMMALS

A good place to see black-and-white ruffed lemurs, white-fronted brown lemurs and mouse lemurs. Sightings of aye-ayes were once regular, but are now far less frequent following cyclone damage to favoured feeding trees. Also good for the greater hedgehog tenrec and Commerson's leaf-nosed bat.

BIRDS

Not particularly diverse or abundant. Madagascar paradise flycatchers, Madagascar bulbuls and Madagascar malachite kingfishers are common. There are sizable heronries around the shoreline including dark phase dimorphic egrets. On the coastal rocks look for Madagascar pratincoles.

REPTILES AND FROGS

The best place in Madagascar to see the leaf-tailed gecko (*Uroplatus fimbriatus*), which is common. Also: pygmy stump-tailed chameleons (*Brookesia peyrierasi* and *B. superciliaris*), panther chameleon, several day geckos (*Phelsuma* spp) and plated lizards (*Zonosaurus madagascariensis* and *Z. brygooi*). Frogs include green-backed (climbing) mantella and *Platypelis grandis*.

Visitor Information

The island lies 5km from Maroantsetra – 30mins by boat. Accessible all year round, but caution is advised in the cyclone season (Jan–Mar) as the sea can be very choppy. There is a well-maintained campsite behind the beach, with sheltered tent platforms, a cold shower (fed from a waterfall) and flush toilets. There are some flat trails, but those which deviate from the shoreline are steep and can be very slippery after rain. A day trip from Maroantsetra is possible, but at least one night's camping is recommended.

ANJOZOROBE FOREST

This increasingly popular rainforest is managed by the NGO FANAMBY. The Anjozorobe–Angavo Forest Corridor represents one of the last vestiges of rainforest remaining in the central plateau. It was first protected in 2005 and should become a reserve by 2015. There are 11 species of lemur and it is also rich in birdlife with more than 80 species observed thus far, as well as a similar number of amphibians and reptiles, more than 25 small mammals, and 550 types of plants including 75 orchids.

Habitat and Terrain

The forest corridor covers 52,200ha and stretches for over 80km. The reserve itself has half a dozen hiking trails ranging in length from one hour to a full day. It is especially rewarding for night walks, with regularly seen highlights being both the mossy and satanic leaf-tailed geckos. On a community-focused circuit you can meet local villagers and participate in tree planting as part of a sustainable development project.

Leaf-tailed gecko, *Uroplatus fimbriatus* (see page 120) (BL)

The striking satanic leaf-tailed gecko (NG)

Key Species

MAMMALS
Indri, diademed sifaka, grey bamboo lemur, eastern woolly lemur, Goodman's mouse lemur and of particular interest is a locally endemic rodent, the eastern vaolavo (*Vaolavo antsahabensis*).

BIRDS
Meller's duck, Madagascar rail, Madagascar snipe, slender-billed flufftail, red-breasted coua, rufous-headed ground-roller, grey emutail, brown emutail, Madagascar yellow-brow and common sunbird-asity.

REPTILES AND FROGS
Nose-horned chameleon (*Calumma nasutum*), globe-horned chameleon (*Calumma globifer*), mossy leaf-tailed gecko (*Uroplatus sikorae*), satanic leaf-tailed gecko (*U. phantasticus*) and Boulenger's forest snake (*Compsophis boulengeri*).

18

Visitor Information

Anjozorobe is situated some 90km (3hrs) northeast of Antananarivo. There are two excellent lodges serving the area, both offering accommodation in tented bungalows.

ANDASIBE-MANTADIA NATIONAL PARK AND SURROUNDS

There is now a cluster of excellent protected areas around the village of Andasibe. Most accessible is the 1,500ha forest of Analamazaotra, of which half is managed by MNP as a special reserve and half administered by the inspiring local community-run Association Mitsinjo. The former part is amalgamated with the much larger Mantadia forest, some 4km north of the village, and collectively known as Andasibe-Mantadia National Park. In combination, the area is perhaps Madagascar's premier rainforest destination, offering close encounters with various lemurs and an opportunity to glimpse some of the island's highly sought-after rarities. Analamazaotra forest remains *the* place to see and hear the indri, and there are also reintroduced diademed sifakas. Unlike the national park, the Mitsinjo-

The eerie wailing call of the indri (see page 59) can be heard at Andasibe. (NG)

managed portion of forest permits night walks – highly recommended if you have time, especially as there is a good chance of seeing the enigmatic hairy-eared dwarf lemur. Mantadia is also rewarding for diademed sifakas and indri, as well as black-and-white ruffed lemurs and four species of ground-roller.

Visitors who have an interest in rare, marsh-dwelling birds and localised amphibians can visit the remaining fragments of Torotorofotsy marsh (also under the management of Mitsinjo), situated west of Mantadia. To see as much of the area's wildlife as possible, a visit to Vohimana is worthwhile too. This rainforest 5km to the east of Andasibe is roughly the same size as Analamazaotra but with a greater range of elevations (700–1,080m). Vohimana has very rewarding night walk prospects for those interested in reptiles and frogs, while in the day diademed sifakas are easily seen.

Habitat and Terrain

The Analamazaotra forest constitutes a fragment of mid-altitude montane rainforest, between 930m and 1,040m. Many of the largest trees have been removed and the canopy does not exceed 20–5m. Dominant trees include species of *Tambourissa*, *Symphonia*, *Dalbergia* and *Weinmannia*. The main indri area in the special reserve is centred on a ridge with some steep slopes descending to a small dammed lake, Lac Vert.

Mantadia is a superb example of lowland and mid-altitude rainforest lying between 800m and 1,260m and covering some 16,000ha. In the valleys, towering buttress-rooted trees rise to 35m. The understorey is dominated by tree ferns (*Cyathea* spp) and *Pandanus* species near watercourses. Orchids and other epiphytes are plentiful. At higher elevations the forest is more stunted and moss and lichen growth is luxuriant. There is little flat ground, with much of the forest steeply inclined. Annual rainfall averages 1,500–2,000mm.

Vohimana has a steep, rainforest-clad gorge and while the core of the rainforest is in good condition at time of writing, there has been significant recent degradation on its outskirts due to logging and forest clearance by means of *tavy* (slash and burn).

Key Species

MAMMALS

Indri, diademed sifaka, common brown lemur, red-bellied lemur, black-and-white ruffed lemur (Mantadia), grey bamboo lemur, Goodman's mouse lemur, eastern woolly lemur, weasel sportive lemur, furry-eared dwarf lemur, hairy-eared dwarf lemur, lowland streaked tenrec, eastern red forest rat and eastern ring-tailed vontsira. A population of the critically endangered greater bamboo lemurs (*Prolemur simus*) was discovered at Torotorofotsy not long ago.

BIRDS

Blue coua, red-fronted coua, blue vanga, red-tailed vanga, nuthatch vanga, tylas vanga, white-headed vanga, velvet asity, common sunbird-asity, pitta-like ground-roller, rufous-headed ground-roller, scaly ground-roller (Mantadia), short-legged ground-roller (Mantadia), Madagascar cuckoo-roller, collared nightjar, Madagascar long-eared owl and cryptic warbler.

At Torotorofotsy, almost all the endemics of the central and eastern domain wetlands can be seen, as can the rare slender-billed flufftail and Meller's duck as well as Madagascar snipe, Madagascar rail, Madagascar swamp warbler and grey emutail.

REPTILES AND FROGS

Parson's chameleon (*Calumma parsonii*), short-horned chameleon, short-nosed chameleon (*C. gastrotaenia*), lance-nosed chameleon (*Calumma gallus*; Vohimana), nose-horned chameleon and *C. malthe*. Also: stump-tailed chameleon (*Brookesia superciliaris*), mossy leaf-tailed gecko (*Uroplatus sikorae*) and Madagascar tree boa. Frogs include the painted mantella (*Mantella madagascariensis*) in Mantadia and numerous others especially species of the genus *Boophis*.

The golden mantella (see page 135) is locally endemic at Torotorofotsy. (NG/NPL)

The small fragments of *Pandanus* and ericoid thicket remaining at Torotorofotsy are home to the unmistakeable golden mantella (*M. aurantiaca*), the country's flagship amphibian, plus at least 40 other frog species.

Visitor Information

Easy to reach by road from Antananarivo (4hrs). Mantadia is an hour's drive along a dirt road from Andasibe. One of Madagascar's top sites, with potential to see ten or more lemur species. An extensive network of easy to moderate paths runs through the Analamazaotra forests. At Mantadia, some circuits can be difficult with steeper slopes and often wet conditions. A two-day visit with night walks is adequate to see Andasibe. With patience, good views of indri are virtually guaranteed. Mantadia warrants more time, ideally two or three early-morning trips. Areas close to the PK14 kilometre post are renowned for the diademed sifaka and indri; either side of the road at PK15 is the best place to look for black-and-white ruffed lemurs, although they can often be very tough to track down. There are now more than a dozen lodges and guesthouses in the immediate area of Andasibe village to suit all budgets.

A rainforest stream at Ranomafana National Park (DA)

RANOMAFANA NATIONAL PARK

This beautiful park was established in 1991 to protect the newly discovered golden bamboo lemur. It has subsequently become one of the most important wildlife sites in Madagascar and its pleasant climate, waterfalls, picturesque rushing river, and huge diversity of species, make it a deserved favourite.

This is one of the best places to see lemurs: at least 12 species are present, many of which are easily seen around the main trail systems (although some sport research collars). The forests here are also excellent for birds, which are diverse; many rainforest endemics are often spotted, but they can be difficult to locate. Reptiles, frogs and invertebrates are also abundant and new species are still being discovered. It is also the easiest place to see giraffe-necked weevils (see page 145).

As of 2012, the site is also home to Centre ValBio, a state-of-the-art scientific research hub and laboratory hosting dozens of students, both foreign and Malagasy. The centre offers tourists the opportunity to take a tour of the facilities and learn about current projects or attend evening lectures presenting some of the latest conservation studies being undertaken.

Also worth a visit is Ranomafana Arboretum, opened in 2007 some 9km east of the park entrance. It offers the opportunity to learn about the region's diverse and fascinating flora and has an especially impressive collection of palms and around 100 native trees. Trilingual signs explain the plants' uses in construction, agriculture and traditional medicine. It belongs to the local community and is managed by volunteers with assistance from a Malagasy NGO.

Habitat and Terrain

Ranomafana's protected montane rainforest covers an area of 41,600ha at altitudes between 600m and 1,400m. The area is dominated by the Namorona River which, fed by many streams, plunges from the eastern escarpment close to the park entrance. The steep slopes are covered with a mixture of primary and secondary forest; much of the secondary growth is dominated by dense stands of introduced Chinese guava (*Psidium cattleyanum*) as well as clumps of giant bamboo (*Cathariostachys madagascariensis*). The average annual rainfall is 2,600mm.

If you are fit and prepared to do a full day's walk then the longer circuits penetrating deep into the primary forest are highly recommended.

Key Species
MAMMALS

Most notable lemurs are the golden bamboo lemur, greater bamboo lemur, Ranomafana grey bamboo lemur, Milne-Edwards' sifaka, red-bellied lemur, red-fronted brown lemur, black-and-white ruffed lemur, Peyrieras' woolly lemur and brown mouse lemur. Other mammals include the spotted fanaloka, eastern ring-tailed vontsira, and eastern and lowland red forest rats.

BIRDS

Of particular interest are the brown mesite, Pollen's vanga, blue vanga, velvet asity, common sunbird-asity, yellow-bellied sunbird-asity, pitta-like ground-roller, scaly ground-roller, short-legged ground-roller, rufous-headed ground-roller, red-fronted coua, Henst's goshawk, collared nightjar, forest rock-thrush, grey-crowned greenbul, wedge-tailed jery and yellow-browed oxylabes.

Golden bamboo lemur
(see page 72) (NG)

23

REPTILES AND FROGS

Parson's chameleon, O'Shaughnessy's chameleon (*Calumma oshaughnessyi*), blue-legged chameleon (*C. crypticum*), stump-tailed chameleons (eg: *Brookesia nasus* and *B. superciliaris*), Madagascar tree boa, at least three leaf-tailed geckos (*Uroplatus sikorae, U. ebenaui* and *U. phantasticus*), peacock day gecko (*Phelsuma quadriocellata*) and numerous frogs. Two very similar mantella frogs are also found here: painted mantella and *Mantella baroni*.

Visitor Information

The park is on the road that connects Fianarantsoa with Mananjary on the east coast. Now that the road is surfaced, the journey from Fianarantsoa takes one hour. An extensive system of well-maintained trails and paths runs through the best wildlife areas, but many are steep and often muddy. April to May and September to December are the best times to visit.

A recommended minimum stay of two nights allows two daytime excursions to Talatakely and one nocturnal stroll to see chameleons, frogs and mouse lemurs. For enthusiasts, three or four days are necessary to see the mid-altitude and higher altitude areas (Vohiparara), which are also excellent at night for frogs and reptiles. There are around 15 hotels including a couple of reasonably comfortable lodges.

Pelican spiders, such as this one seen at Ranomafana, are uniquely adapted to catching fellow spiders; see page 154. (PB)

Characteristic of the Menabe protected area, Grandidier's baobab is the largest of Madagascar's six endemic baobab species. The Avenue of Baobabs (*above*) is now a national monument. (AVZ)

DECIDUOUS FORESTS/
SEASONALLY DRY FORESTS

The deciduous forests of western and northern Madagascar are less diverse than the rainforests of the east, but nonetheless contain a wealth of flora and fauna of great significance, including some of Madagascar's most endangered animals. The level of endemism (around 90%) is higher than in the east, although the species diversity is somewhat lower.

Canopy height and tree density is lower than in eastern rainforests, giving the forests a more open feel. The large trees have adapted to a prolonged dry season by shedding their leaves to prevent moisture loss through evaporation. Some, like the baobabs that are such a feature of this region, store water in their bulbous trunks, hence the name 'bottle trees'. Others have roots that are swollen with water to tide them over in times of drought.

Forests are described as having storeys or layers of vegetation showing different characteristics. Seasonally dry western forests have an understorey comprising dense shrubs and saplings, many of which retain their leaves during the rainless months, and an overstorey of large trees up to 20m tall, which lose their leaves in the dry season.

Deciduous forest is found on the coastal plains and associated limestone plateaux from sea level to 800m, stretching from Antsiranana at the island's northern tip to Morombe on the west coast. Like the eastern rainforests, they have been ravaged by man and are now only found in discontinuous patches, being replaced in between by largely sterile coarse savanna grassland. This destruction is of particular concern since the trees here grow extremely slowly. The dry season extends from May to October, but annual rainfall varies considerably: from 500mm in the southwest to 2,000mm in the far north.

Several major protected areas exist within the deciduous forest zone. While some are remote and remain difficult for visitors to reach, others are among the most popular and rewarding wildlife-watching localities on the island.

Of particular note are parks incorporating limestone massifs that have been eroded into spectacular pinnacle formations known as karst or *tsingy*. Rivers flowing through these areas have eroded underground passages and caves. Some have subsequently collapsed to form canyons, within which deciduous forest flourishes, often supporting isolated faunal communities unlike any others on the island. Wildlife-watching can be especially rewarding in such areas: the main examples are at Ankarana, Bemaraha and Namoroka, although the last is not easily accessible.

Choosing the best time to visit the western forests is difficult. By far the most pleasant months climatically are May to September when it is dry and relatively cool, but wildlife is less active. As the rainy season progresses so the heat and humidity rise and insects, particularly flies, become increasingly persistent. When the discomfort is at its worst, from December to March, the wildlife (especially reptiles) is at its best. Overall, late September to December is the most rewarding period.

The Tsingy Rary at Ankarana (DA)

ANKARANA NATIONAL PARK

Once only the preserve of adventure-seekers, Ankarana is now accessible to any reasonably fit visitors willing to camp or stay in the rustic accommodation outside the reserve. The rewards are high, with a dramatic landscape of limestone pinnacle karst (*tsingy*), huge caves, untouched forest and a wealth of wildlife.

Habitat and Terrain

The Ankarana Massif is a limestone plateau approximately 5km by 20km, rising abruptly from the surrounding grassy plain. It is dominated by impressive *tsingy* formations that form an almost impenetrable fortress in places. There is an extensive subterranean cave system with underground rivers, and isolated canyons where caves have collapsed. Moist deciduous forest grows around the periphery and penetrates into the larger canyons. The canopy reaches 25m, with dominant trees including species of *Cassia*, *Dalbergia*, *Ficus* and baobab (*Adansonia madagascariensis* and *A. perrieri*). Annual rainfall in the reserve averages 1,800mm.

Key Species

MAMMALS
Crowned lemur, Sanford's brown lemur, Ankarana sportive lemur and northern rufous mouse lemur. Also northern ring-tailed vontsira, spotted fanaloka and fosa. The caves make this a haven for bats with at least 16 species recorded.

BIRDS
White-breasted mesite, crested coua, hook-billed vanga, Madagascar crested ibis, Madagascar pygmy kingfisher, Madagascar harrier hawk and Madagascar scops owl.

REPTILES
Oustalet's chameleon (*Furcifer oustaleti*), panther chameleon, Petter's white-lipped chameleon (*F. petteri*), big-headed geckos (*Paroedura* spp), leaf-tailed geckos, (*Uroplatus henkeli* and *U. ebenaui*), giant day gecko and Madagascar ground boa (*Acrantophis madagascariensis*).

Visitor Information

The park's main (eastern) gate is 108km south of Antsiranana on Route Nationale 6. Campsites can be reached by 4x4, but some visitors prefer the 3hr hike from Mahamasina village at the road, where there are two nice lodges and simple accommodation options; another comfortable lodge is to be found at the park's western entrance. The trails are moderate to difficult; access is easiest during the drier months (May–Nov).

It can be very hot during the day, but cool at night. Campement Anilotra is best for lemurs and small carnivores. Areas close to the camp at Mahamasina can be good for sightings of the elusive fosa.

Crowned lemur, female (see page 67) (DS)

The golden-crowned sifaka (see page 63) is one of the most endangered lemur species. (NG)

DARAINA AREA

Currently, this sensitive area is not government-protected, but there are plans to create a national park. Meanwhile the Malagasy NGO FANAMBY is working with the local communities to conserve the forest. The principal reason for the region's biological importance is the golden-crowned sifaka, found only here.

Habitat and Terrain

The area is a mosaic of rolling hills covered with patches of deciduous forest, semi-evergreen forest and gallery forest, interspersed with large areas of degraded grassland, dry scrub and agricultural land. The forests are highly fragmented, covering a total area of only 44,000ha, with each of the individual forest blocks no larger than 14,000ha.

Key Species

MAMMALS

Principally golden-crowned sifaka by day and the elusive aye-aye by night; also crowned lemur, Sanford's brown lemur, Daraina sportive lemur, fork-marked lemur, dwarf lemur, mouse lemur, fosa and greater hedgehog tenrec. Night walks can be particularly rewarding as aye-ayes are seen with increasing regularity.

BIRDS

Van Dam's vanga, hook-billed vanga, sickle-billed vanga, crested coua, Madagascar crested ibis and Madagascar harrier hawk.

REPTILES

Oustalet's chameleon, panther chameleon, fish-scaled gecko (*Geckolepis* sp), big-headed gecko (*Paroedura stumpffi*), giant day gecko and Madagascar ground boa.

Visitor Information

The town of Daraina lies 70km to the west of Iharana (Vohemar), off the road to Ambilobe on the west coast. The road is poor and passable only during drier months (May–Dec). There are no facilities within the forest, but there's one simple but comfortable lodge at Daraina. It can be very hot during the day and walking is moderately tough-going. The best forests for the golden-crowned sifaka are adjacent to the village of Andranotsimaty, 5km northeast of Daraina. For advice contact FANAMBY (*www.association-fanamby.org*).

ANJAJAVY PRIVATE RESERVE

Located on the remote northwest coast, this private hotel and reserve complex is an oasis for both wildlife and visitors. This fascinating area comprises coastal mangroves, limestone outcrops and seasonally dry deciduous forest, interspersed with pockets of cultivated land. In forest areas, many of the lemurs, birds and reptiles have become tolerant of humans and are easy to see. The coastal limestone has been eroded into intricate formations and caves. One of the caves contains subfossil skulls and bones of extinct giant lemurs embedded in the rocks.

Habitat and Terrain

Along the coast, golden sandy beaches mix with dramatic limestone outcrops and mangrove-fringed estuaries. Inland grows typical seasonally dry deciduous forest, dominated by *Dalbergia*, *Hidegardia* and *Commiphora* species, as well as an abundance of baobab trees.

Key Species
MAMMALS
Coquerel's sifaka, common brown lemur, mouse lemurs, sportive lemur (species to be confirmed), Madagascar flying fox, greater hedgehog tenrec and fosa.

Coastal deciduous forest near Anjajavy (NG)

BIRDS

Many endemics are easy to see. Coastal excursions provide excellent opportunities for sighting the Madagascar fish eagle and the rare Madagascar sacred ibis. Other species include: Madagascar crested ibis, greater vasa parrot, grey-headed lovebird, red-capped coua, Coquerel's coua, crested coua, Madagascar green pigeon, sickle-billed vanga and Madagascar pygmy kingfisher.

REPTILES

Oustalet's chameleon, collared iguanid (*Oplurus cuvieri*), fish-scaled gecko, Madagascar giant day gecko, Madagascar ground boa and Madagascar hognose snake (*Leioheterodon madagascariensis*).

Visitor Information

Anjajavy is accessible only by 1½hr private flight (expensive) from Antananarivo. The hotel is situated on a small peninsula adjacent to beautiful sandy beaches and bays with pockets of deciduous forest and mangroves immediately to hand. A stay of three or four nights is recommended, including a coastal excursion to Moromba Bay to see wonderful coastal baobab forest and Madagascar fish eagles.

SAHAMALAZA–ILES RADAMA NATIONAL PARK

Inaugurated in 2007, this is one of the country's newest national parks, contained within one of Madagascar's three UNESCO Biosphere Reserves. The 26,000ha park includes both terrestrial habitats in the Sahamalaza region of the northwest, and marine parcels amongst the Radama Islands archipelago.

Habitat and Terrain

A diverse range of habitats is protected by this park, including a transition between seasonally dry western deciduous and evergreen Sambirano forest types. The forests cover approximately 11,000ha, much of it in a disturbed condition. There are extensive mangroves (10,000ha) in which all eight of Madagascar's mangrove tree species can be found.

Reefs in the marine parcels support some 216 species of coral and at least 251 of fish. There are also seagrass beds and mudflats.

Key Species

MAMMALS

Blue-eyed (Sclater's) black lemur, aye-aye, northern bamboo lemur, Sahamalaza sportive lemur, northern giant mouse lemur (*Mirza zaza*) and fosa.

BIRDS

Madagascar crested ibis, Humblot's heron, Madagascar fish eagle, Madagascar buzzard, crested coua, greater vasa parrot, grey-headed lovebird, common jery, Sakalava weaver, and hook-billed and Chabert's vangas.

REPTILES

Oustalet's and panther chameleons, stump-tailed chameleon *Brookesia stumpffi*, collared iguanid, fish-scaled geckos (*Geckolepis maculata* and *G. oviceps*), leaf-tailed geckos (*Uroplatus henkeli* and *U. ebenaui*) and at least ten species of snake have been recorded thus far, but species surveys are still very much a work in progress.

Visitor Information

Although it is still in the nascent stages of development for tourist infrastructure, travellers can already experience several areas. A simple campsite was established in the park in 2012 and an exclusive upmarket lodge just offshore on the island of Nosy Saba offers visits by boat. Activities include mangrove boat trips, snorkelling, birding and lemur-watching – particularly for blue-eyed black lemurs in Ankarafa Forest, which has three circuits of varying difficulty (1½–4hrs), the start of which can be reached via a 2–3hr walk inland from Marovato (on the coast opposite Nosy Saba) or in 4hrs by 4x4 from the inland direction on a road that is passable only between May and November. The park office is at Maromandia.

Coquerel's sifaka (see page 61) (DA)

ANKARAFANTSIKA NATIONAL PARK

Ankarafantsika (formerly Ampijoroa) competes with Kirindy as the most rewarding western seasonally dry deciduous forest. Access is straightforward and there is basic comfortable accommodation.

A clear network of level paths makes wildlife-viewing easy. Many groups of lemurs have become habituated so can be observed at close quarters. Night walks in adjacent forests are particularly rewarding as the density of nocturnal lemurs is high. Birdwatching is also outstanding with a number of rare western endemics frequently seen.

Habitat and Terrain

The park is a mixture of deciduous forest and a karstic limestone plateau covering 65,520ha. The main road connecting Mahajanga with Antananarivo cuts through the western portion of the park providing easy access. Lac Ravelobe lies to the east of the road and on sandy soils around the lake grows typical deciduous forest with a canopy height of 15–20m. The understorey is sparse, with virtually no epiphytes but abundant lianas. In open rocky areas succulents like *Pachypodium rosulatum* and *Aloe* species grow. The terrain is mostly fairly flat. Annual rainfall is 1,000–500mm.

Key Species
MAMMALS
Coquerel's sifaka, mongoose lemur, common brown lemur, western woolly lemur, Milne-Edwards' sportive lemur, fat-tailed dwarf lemur, grey mouse lemur and golden-brown mouse lemur. Other mammals include the fosa, western tuft-tailed rat, long-tailed big-footed mouse, Commerson's leaf-nosed bat, tomb bat and the introduced small Indian civet (*Viverricula indica*).

BIRDS
The best place to see western specialties such as the Madagascar fish eagle, Van Dam's vanga, Schlegel's asity and white-breasted mesite. Also: red-capped coua, Coquerel's coua, crested coua, Madagascar green pigeon, rufous vanga, sickle-billed vanga, greater vasa parrot and Madagascar pygmy kingfisher.

REPTILES
Abundant, with a greater variety seen during the wet season. Oustalet's chameleon, rhinoceros chameleon (*Furcifer rhinoceratus*), stump-tailed chameleons (including *Brookesia stumpffi* and *B. decaryi*), iguanids (*Oplurus cuvieri* and *O. cyclurus*), leaf-tailed geckos (*Uroplatus henkeli* and *U. guentheri*), fish-scaled gecko, Madagascar ground boa, Madagascar hognose snake, spear-nosed snake (*Langaha madagascariensis*) and *fandrefiala* (*Ithycyphus miniatus*). The lake is home to Nile crocodiles. There is a captive-breeding programme for the ploughshare tortoise (*angonoka*), flat-tailed tortoise (*kapidolo*) and Madagascar big-headed (side-necked) turtle (*Erymnochelys madagascariensis*), run by the Durrell Wildlife Conservation Trust.

Visitor Information
By good road, 2hrs from Mahajanga. Bungalows and sheltered tent pitches are available and the local guides are generally excellent. Trails on both sides of road (*Jardin Botanique A* and *B*) are wide and easy to walk. Reptiles are more visible after the first rains in November. In summer (Dec–Mar) it can be extremely hot.

TSINGY DE BEMARAHA NATIONAL PARK
This remote and thrilling limestone region is a World Heritage Site covering 152,000ha, the southern half being the national park. It is the second largest protected area on the island. An extensive area of limestone massif has been eroded into Madagascar's largest and most impressive pinnacle karst (*tsingy*).

Habitat and Terrain
The razor-sharp *tsingy* form an impenetrable fortress in places, and at the park's

Several circuits using boardwalks and suspension bridges allow the *tsingy* to be explored on foot. (IM)

southern edge the Manambolo River cuts a spectacular gorge through the limestone. Around the karst grows deciduous forest dominated by *Dalbergia*, *Commiphora* and *Hildegardia* species. There are numerous succulents including *Kalanchoe* and *Pachypodium* species, and in shady canyons *Pandanus* and ferns flourish.

Key Species
MAMMALS
Decken's sifaka, red-fronted brown lemur, Cleese's woolly lemur, grey mouse lemur, western rufous mouse lemur, fat-tailed dwarf lemur, Randrianasolo's sportive lemur, aye-aye, western ring-tailed vontsira (*Galidia elegans occidentalis*), fosa and western red forest rat. Arguably the single richest site for bats in Madagascar; around half of the island's species occur here.

BIRDS
Specials include Coquerel's coua, red-capped coua, crested coua, sickle-billed vanga, white-headed vanga, rufous vanga, Madagascar green pigeon, greater vasa parrot and Madagascar pygmy kingfisher. Madagascar's most recently described bird, the tsingy wood rail (*Mentocrex beankaensis*), is endemic to the area.

REPTILES
Madagascar ground boa, stump-tailed chameleon (*Brookesia perarmata*), leaf-tailed geckos (*Uroplatus guentheri*, *U. henkeli* and *U. ebenaui*) and big-headed gecko (*Paroedura tanjaka*).

Visitor Information
Access is via Bekopaka on the north bank of the Manambolo River. This is a 5hr drive from Belo-sur-Tsiribihina, which in turn is a further 5hr drive from Morondava or may alternatively be reached from Miandrivazo by a three-day descent of the River Tsiribihina. Access is only feasible during dry season (May–Nov) when the road is passable. There is a system of trails and boardwalks over the *tsingy* beginning at the park entrance. The circuits are moderate to difficult and vary in length from two to eight hours. The best areas for wildlife lie within the forest close to the entrance. There is an increasing range of accommodation from camping to comfortable hotels. Given the considerable effort required to reach Bemaraha, a stay of at least three nights is advisable.

KIRINDY FOREST
This can be one of the most rewarding wildlife locations in Madagascar, yet it has only relatively recently received official conservation as part of the Menabe Protected Area. Although previously logged, Kirindy remains the best place to see a number of endemic dry forest species like the giant jumping rat, northern bokiboky (*Mungotictis decemlineata*), fosa and Madame Berthe's mouse lemur.

Male fosa (see page 84). Kirindy remains the best place to see the island's largest carnivore. It is regularly seen around the campsite (Oct–Dec). (NG)

The giant jumping rat (see page 90) is now restricted to a narrow band of coastal forest between the rivers Tomitsy and Tsiribihina. (NG)

Habitat and Terrain

Kirindy comprises some 10,000ha of deciduous forest growing on sandy soils of the western coastal plain. The tree species are similar to other western deciduous forests, with a canopy height typically of 12–15m, reaching 20–5m in more humid areas along watercourses. Beneath the canopy, throughout much of the forest, the understorey and intermediate layer are densely vegetated. Three species of baobab live here: *Adansonia rubrostipa*, *A. za* and *A. grandidieri*, the last being the largest of the baobabs, sometimes exceeding 30m in height. Annual rainfall is 700–800mm, with the majority falling between December and March.

Key Species

MAMMALS

Madame Berthe's mouse lemur, grey mouse lemur, red-tailed sportive lemur, pale fork-marked lemur, Coquerel's giant dwarf lemur, fat-tailed dwarf lemur, Verreaux's sifaka, red-fronted brown lemur, fosa, northern bokiboky, giant jumping rat, western big-footed mouse, common tenrec, greater and lesser hedgehog tenrecs, and large-eared tenrec.

BIRDS

Highlights include white-breasted mesite, Coquerel's coua, crested coua, sickle-billed vanga, white-headed vanga, rufous vanga, blue vanga, Chabert's vanga, Madagascar cuckoo-roller, Madagascar harrier hawk, Henst's goshawk, banded kestrel, and both lesser and greater vasa parrots.

REPTILES

Flat-tailed tortoise, Madagascar ground boa, Madagascar hognose snake, speckled hognose snake (*Leioheterodon geayi*), spear-nosed snake, plated lizard (*Zonosaurus karsteni*), Oustalet's chameleon, Labord's chameleon (*Furcifer labordi*), leaf-tailed gecko (*Uroplatus guentheri*), big-headed geckos (*Paroedura picta* and *P. bastardi*) and several day geckos including *Phelsuma kochi* and *P. mutabilis*.

Visitor Information

Within easy reach by road of Morondava. The 2½hr drive is via the Avenue of Baobabs, now a National Monument (see page 25). Trails within the forest are mainly broad and flat.

Wildlife-watching is best in spring and summer (Oct–Apr), particularly after rain, but January to April can be hot and humid. However, in the cooler months many species are aestivating. If you visit in November you may hit the jackpot and watch the extraordinary spectacle of fosas mating.

There are simple bungalows and dormitory accommodation with a snack bar serving drinks and simple meals. Two or three nights' stay is recommended to make the most of the nocturnal opportunities.

ZOMBITSE NATIONAL PARK

Together with the adjacent forests of Vohibasia, Zombitse constitutes the last – and therefore biologically significant – remnant of transition forest between the western and southern regions.

It covers 17,240ha. The forest margins have been continually eroded by fires and the spread of agriculture, although formal protection has recently reduced this. Zombitse is of particular interest to birdwatchers, being home to one of the country's rarest endemics, Appert's greenbul.

Zombitse park entrance (DA)

36

Habitat and Terrain

Zombitse is similar in appearance to western deciduous forests; the canopy averages 15m, the terrain is flat, and the soil sandy. Many species are shared with areas further south, including baobabs (*Adansonia za*). Annual rainfall averages 700mm with a long dry season (May–Oct) and no permanent watercourses.

Key Species
MAMMALS

Verreaux's sifaka, ring-tailed lemur, red-fronted brown lemur, Hubbard's sportive lemur, pale fork-marked lemur, Coquerel's giant dwarf lemur, fat-tailed dwarf lemur, grey mouse lemur, fosa, greater hedgehog tenrec, large-eared tenrec and western big-footed mouse.

BIRDS

An excellent birding site; in particular people come to seek the locally endemic Appert's greenbul as well as the giant coua, crested coua, Madagascar cuckoo-roller, white-headed vanga and white-browed owl.

REPTILES

The locally endemic Standing's day gecko (*Phelsuma standingi*), Oustalet's chameleon (particularly large individuals) and Dumeril's boa (*Acrantophis dumerili*).

Aerangis ellisii orchid (DA)

Visitor Information

The park straddles Route Nationale 7, some 25km east of Sakaraha. It is easily reached from Ranohira (1hr) or Toliara (3hrs). Circuits start at the park office and easy to moderate trails lead into the forest on both sides of road. Accessible year-round (best Oct–Apr). Most visitors stop *en route* between Isalo and Toliara. It is possible to see lemurs such as Verreaux's sifakas and red-fronted brown lemurs in trees close to the road.

Baobabs and thorny *Didierea* trees near the Mikea forest, between Ifaty and Morombe. (JB)

THE SOUTHERN REGION

The spiny bush (commonly, but somewhat misleadingly, also called spiny *forest*) comprises some of the most distinctive and unusual vegetation in Madagascar.

The south is the harshest and most arid part of the island, and consequently there is a lower diversity of flora and fauna than in other regions. But endemism is very high; about 95% of the plant species are found nowhere else. The spiny bush is a deciduous thicket dominated by members of the Didiereaceae and Euphorbiaceae families. It stretches from Morombe on the west coast around the southern coastline almost as far as Taolagnaro, and extends up to 50km inland.

Didiereaceae look rather like cacti and are an excellent example of convergent evolution. Nature has independently arrived at similar water-retaining, predator-deterring methods of survival in these two unrelated plant groups living in dry climates continents apart. Despite the superficial resemblance, the thorns of Didiereaceae are adaptations of the stem, unlike the spines of a cactus which are in fact modified leaves. Amongst the four genera of Didiereaceae are euphorbias. Most ooze a poisonous latex (which can cause temporary blindness) if cut or damaged and only a few species bear thorns. Although members of these two families dominate throughout, there is considerable variation across the spiny bush band from Ifaty in the west to Andohahela in the east.

Conspicuous among these strange plants are the so-called bottle trees. These include baobabs (*Adansonia* spp), which tower above the thickets, and species of *Pachypodium* or 'elephant's foot': some really do look like elephant's feet, being squat and grey, while others resemble prickly bottles. In combination, these elements create one of the world's most fascinating landscapes.

Being so arid, this area has suffered relatively little from slash-and-burn agriculture. Nonetheless, the forests are becoming increasingly fragmented with intensified pressures for charcoal, maize cultivation and building materials. Only small areas of spiny bush are officially protected, but plans are afoot to create a national park north of Ifaty, an area home to some highly localised and threatened birds, reptiles and plants.

Gallery forest (also called riverine or tamarind forest) occurs along many southern rivers. This is superficially similar to western deciduous forest, but is dominated by tamarind trees (*Tamarindus indica*) known locally as *kily*, which may exceed 20m. There are also sprawling banyan trees (*Ficus* spp) as well as an understorey of shrubs and saplings. The private reserve of Berenty is mainly gallery forest, though there is a small parcel of spiny bush as well.

Coral ragg scrub and mangrove at St Augustine's Bay south of Toliara (AD)

Pic d'Imarivolanitra, Andringitra's highest peak, formerly known as Pic Boby (NG)

ANDRINGITRA NATIONAL PARK

Centred on Madagascar's second highest peak, Pic d'Imarivolanitra, Andringitra is unusual in straddling both eastern and western habitats. The eastern slopes are typical mid-altitude rainforest but have not been developed for tourism. The majority of the park lies on the western slopes and this unique region of granite and gneiss formations, high-altitude vegetation, forest and waterfalls, offers some of the best trekking opportunities in Madagascar. The rainforest areas support the greatest diversity of wildlife (very similar to Ranomafana), while the drier western side is less varied, but nevertheless supports interesting species.

Habitat and Terrain

Andringitra covers 31,200ha, but significant variations in altitude (650–2,658m) mean that the flora and fauna vary, with vegetation ranging from humid forests to grasslands (with 30 species of terrestrial orchid) and high alpine heather-like formations, and from a spectacular rocky zone to the frosty summit of Pic d'Imarivolanitra. While some of the trails are relatively short and easy, others are long and steep in parts. The climb to the summit is strenuous.

Key Species

MAMMALS

Most notable is a distinct form (ecotype) of ring-tailed lemur that is adapted to high altitudes; it is more densely furred and browner in colour than ring-tails found elsewhere. The highland streaked tenrec is common.

BIRDS

Madagascar kestrel, Madagascar buzzard, Madagascar coucal, Madagascar lesser cuckoo, Madagascar hoopoe, Madagascar bulbul and forest rock-thrush.

REPTILES AND FROGS

Diverse in the rainforest; less so on the western slopes and at high elevations. Montane jewel chameleon (*Furcifer campani*) and plated lizards (*Zonosaurus madagascariensis*, *Z. ornatus* and *Z. aeneus*). Amphibians include the burrowing frogs *Scaphiophryne madagascariensis* and *S. spinosa*.

Visitor Information

Reached by road, 46km south of Ambalavao. Two well-established camps offer comfortable accommodation. There are two entrances: Namoly (1hr drive by private vehicle from Ambalavao) and Morarano (at the park's western perimeter). The winter months (May–Oct) are very cold at night but comfortable for walking. Wild flowers are best in the warm, wet season. The easiest trail is the beautiful 3hr hike to the sacred waterfall, but the tougher Diavolana trail (a 7hr circuit) has splendid views and varied scenery. The trek up Pic d'Imarivolanitra provides the ultimate views.

ISALO NATIONAL PARK

Isalo is quite unlike any other place in Madagascar. Its appeal is the remarkable landscape of eroded ruiniform sandstone outcrops, canyons and rare plants. And the feeling of space. The morning and evening light is often spectacular, making this an attractive place for photographers. It is one of Madagascar's oldest, and most popular, national parks.

Habitat and Terrain

The park covers 81,500ha of the Isalo Massif, which rises majestically from the surrounding flat grassy plain. The sandstone has been eroded into bizarre shapes, cut through by impressive gorges. Vegetation is concentrated in the bottoms of the canyons where streams flow. These wooded areas are dominated by the fire-resistant tapia tree (*Uapaca*

Pachypodium rosulatum gracilis in flower (NG)

bojeri) – on which an endemic Malagasy silkworm feeds – as well as *Pandanus pulcher* and the locally endemic feather palm, *Chrysalidocarpus isaloenses*. On the cliffs and rocks grow several endemic succulents, including the elephant's foot, *Pachypodium rosulatum*, and the Isalo aloe, *Aloe isaloensis*.

Key Species

MAMMALS

In the canyons are ring-tailed lemurs, Verreaux's sifakas and red-fronted brown lemurs.

BIRDS

Benson's rock-thrush, white-throated rail, Madagascar cuckoo-roller, Madagascar coucal, Madagascar wagtail, Madagascar kestrel, Madagascar hoopoe and bat hawk.

The ring-tails of Anja are now habituated enough to guarantee you great photo opportunities. (DA)

REPTILES AND FROGS

Oustalet's chameleon, warty chameleon (*Furcifer verrucosus*), jewel chameleon (*F. lateralis*), spiny-tailed iguanid (*Oplurus quadrimaculatus*), stump-tailed chameleon (*Brookesia brygooi*) and two beautiful locally endemic frogs: *Mantella expectata* and the painted burrowing frog (*Scaphiophryne gottlebei*).

Visitor Information

The park lies on Route Nationale 7 between Fianarantsoa and Toliara, just to the north of the Ranohira. There are reasonably priced accommodation options in this village, and several more lodges of increasing levels of comfort as you head south along the park's eastern boundary. It is best to avoid the wet season (Jan–Mar). From June to August daytime temperatures are pleasant, but nights can be very cold; and between November and March the days may be too hot. From August to early October the elephant's foot plants are in bloom and temperatures are moderate.

Even driving past Isalo gives some idea of its rugged beauty. To see any wildlife, however, you must hike and preferably camp. Hiking can be moderate to difficult. The natural swimming pool, the Piscine Naturelle, is popular and can get very busy. For the best lemur-viewing head for the Canyon des Singes.

ANJA COMMUNITY PARK

About 13km southwest of the town of Ambalavao, set in a region characterised by spectacular granite formations, Anja is a small (30ha) locally managed area where a thriving population of some 300 ring-tailed lemurs finds sanctuary. This is the country's most visited community-run conservation site.

Habitat and Terrain

There are two circuits, the shorter of which takes 1–2hrs to complete. This well-maintained short trail winds past some impressive rocks, topped by waiting lemurs, to a sacred cliff where there is an apparently inaccessible tomb high in the rock face. A longer circuit incorporating several stunning viewpoints can take up to 6hrs.

Key Species

Although the ring-tails are the reason everyone comes here, the herpetofauna deserves a mention too, with chameleons including Oustalet's chameleon, jewel chameleon and even the stump-tailed chameleon *Brookesia brygooi*. Other lizards found here are the iguanid *Oplurus quadrimaculatus* and the plated lizard *Zonosaurus madagascariensis*.

Visitor Information

There are reasonable hotels in Ambalavao, which can help to organise an excursion here. Being located on Route Nationale 7, Anja Park is a popular stop off for tourists driving the length of this classic and deservedly popular route.

IFATY SPINY BUSH AND TOLIARA AREA

Although unprotected, the spiny bush near Ifaty is of great interest to birdwatchers and succulent enthusiasts. The narrow band stretching from Ifaty northwards to the Mangoky River (less than 50 by 180km) encompasses the entire global range of two threatened birds: the long-tailed ground-roller and the subdesert mesite. There is plenty else of interest too, not least an excellent diversity of other birds and some of the most bizarre flora imaginable. The lack of legal protection is starkly visible, with

Long-tailed ground-roller (see page 97) (NG)

tree-felling and charcoal production in evidence throughout the forest. The Reniala Nature Reserve is a small area (45ha) of protected spiny bush which offers excellent birding and is easier to visit than the unprotected habitat.

Whilst in the area, those with botanical or ornithological interests should also visit the 40ha botanical garden called Arboretum d'Antsokay, a few kilometres outside Toliara. It showcases some 900 species of the region's fascinating drought-resistant flora – mostly *Euphorbia* and *Didiera* species, as well as impressive, tall *Pachypodium* and *Aloe* plants.

Habitat and Terrain

Growing on flat sandy coastal soils, the spiny bush is dominated by *Didierea madagascariensis* and *D. trolli*, various *Euphorbia* and *Pachypodium* species, and two species of baobab (*Adansonia rubrostipa* and *A. za*). This is the driest region on the island; what rain there is tends to fall between December and March. Other months are often completely dry.

Key Species

MAMMALS

Not prominent or easily seen. Grey mouse lemur, grey-brown mouse lemur, white-footed sportive lemur and lesser hedgehog tenrec. There have been very occasional sightings of the southern bokiboky (*Mungotictis lineata*).

BIRDS

The most sought-after species are: long-tailed ground-roller, subdesert mesite, Lafresnaye's vanga and banded kestrel. Others frequently seen include: sickle-billed vanga, Archbold's newtonia, thamnornis warbler, subdesert brush warbler, olive-capped coua, running coua and Madagascar plover.

REPTILES

Spider tortoise (*Pyxis arachnoides*), Dumeril's boa, iguanid (*Oplurus cyclurus*), big-headed geckos (*Paroedura bastardi* and *P. picta*), Oustalet's chameleon and horned chameleon (*Furcifer antimena*).

Visitor Information

The spiny bush is inland from the resort villages of Ifaty and Mangily, 29km north from Toliara (as the road is very poor this drive takes 1½hrs). Birdwatching is best in the breeding season (Sep–Dec) when they are more vocal. Outside this period, many birds can be harder to find. Birdwatching has to begin at dawn as it is extremely hot by 09.00. Nocturnal walks are worthwhile for reptiles. A local guide is essential as it is easy to get lost. Reniala Nature Reserve is conveniently close to the Ifaty hotels.

Near to Toliara, Arboretum d'Antsokay is situated on Route Nationale 7 and is perfect for a visit of an hour or two, but also has a few comfy bungalows and a restaurant for those planning more than a passing stop.

Cheeky Grandidier's vontsiras regularly visit the campsites. (NG)

TSIMANAMPETSOTSA NATIONAL PARK

This fabulous 43,200ha national park in far south-west Madagascar is situated some 50km south of the Vezo fishing village of Anakao and includes substantial areas of healthy spiny bush with a remarkable flora of 185 recorded species, chalk caves (some inhabited by blind fish, *Typhleotris madagascariensis*) and a 15km-long milky blue soda lake where greater flamingos occur (Nov–Apr). The lake is classified as a Ramsar site.

Habitat and Terrain

There are five easy circuits. The 45min Andaka trail leads to the lakeside where flamingos can be seen in season. More popular is the 5km Andalamaiky trail, which takes visitors to see numerous spectacular specimens of tall pachypodiums, bloated baobabs (one thought by some to be more than 3,000 years old) and a cave. The 3hr Emande circuit takes you through otherworldly baobab-dominated bush to a panoramic lake view, while to see the blind cave fish the 2hr Tsiamaso bush trail can be done.

The park also has a flooded cave where cave diving is possible. This must be organised through the Atlantis dive centre in Anakao and is only open to experienced divers in small groups.

Key Species
MAMMALS

Ring-tailed lemur, Verreaux's sifaka, grey-brown mouse lemur (*Microcebus griseorufus*), fat-tailed dwarf lemur, white-footed sportive lemur and Grandidier's vontsira.

BIRDS
The impressive 112-strong local species list includes greater flamingo, Humblot's heron, Madagascar plover, Madagascar green pigeon, greater vasa parrot, Verreaux's and running couas, littoral rock-thrush, Archbold's newtonia, and Lafresnaye's and red-shouldered vangas.

REPTILES AND FROGS
Of the 42 recorded species, just three are frogs, including the burrowing frog *Scaphiophryne brevis*. Reptiles include radiated and spider tortoises, day geckos (*Phelsuma breviceps* and *P. mutabilis*), big-headed geckos (*Paroedura picta*, *P. vahiny*, *P. bastardi* and *P. maingoka*), fish-scaled gecko (*Geckolepis typica*), iguanids (*Oplurus quadrimaculatus*, *O. saxicola* and *O. cyclurus*) limbless skinks (*Androngo trivittatus*, *Pygomeles braconnieri* and *Voeltzkowia fierinensis*), Dumeril's boa, Oustalet's chameleon, warty chameleon and jewel chameleon.

Visitor Information
The park can be visited as a long day trip from Anakao, which has a range of comfortable accommodation, or from the nearer village of Ambola – but an overnight stay camping in the park is strongly recommended in order to see the locally plentiful star attraction – Grandidier's vontsira – and other nocturnal wildlife. The vontsiras are quite bold and opportunistic and will raid tents or vehicles for food.

The cave-dwelling fish are blind and largely lack pigment. (NG)

ANDOHAHELA NATIONAL PARK

Lying at the boundary of the southeastern rainforest and the spiny bush, Andohahela spans the east and west sides of the Anosyennes Mountains and a remarkable diversity of habitats. The spiny bush here is quite different in composition from that at Ifaty. Andohahela is a complex of three separate forest areas north west of Taolagnaro. Parcel 3 is easier to visit than Parcels 1 and 2.

Habitat and Terrain

Parcel 1 covers 63,100ha of lowland, mid- and high-altitude rainforest up to 2,000m, representing the southernmost tip of the humid forest band. Parcel 2 covers 12,420ha of largely typical spiny bush – dominated by *Alluaudia procera* and *A. ascendens* – and gallery forest. With the proximity of humid forest, this area acts as a transition zone for many species and is one of Madagascar's most biologically diverse forest areas. Parcel 3 covers just 500ha of the Ambolo Massif and is a representative fragment of transition forest, primarily set aside to protect the locally endemic triangle palm, *Dypsis decaryi*, but is also home to many other species. Troops of ring-tailed lemurs can be seen, sometimes even from the road.

Key Species (spiny bush areas)

MAMMALS

Verreaux's sifaka, ring-tailed lemur, white-footed sportive lemur, grey-brown mouse lemur, grey mouse lemur and lesser hedgehog tenrec.

BIRDS

Hook-billed vanga, sickle-billed vanga, Archbold's newtonia, thamnornis warbler, subdesert brush warbler, olive-capped coua, running coua and Madagascar kestrel.

REPTILES

Radiated tortoise (*Astrochelys radiata*), Dumeril's boa, iguanids (*Oplurus quadrimaculatus* and *O. saxicola*), three-eyed lizard (*Chalaradon madagascariensis*) and Oustalet's chameleon.

Verreaux's sifakas (see page 60) are easy to approach in Andohahela. (NG)

Visitor Information

Both Parcel 2 (Mangatsiaka, Ihazofotsy) and Parcel 3 (Tsimelahy) are easily reached from Taolagnaro. At both locations there are basic campsites and well-marked trail systems. September to December is perhaps the best time to visit. Day trips are possible but overnight stays are better for early morning and nocturnal walks. (There have been problems with banditry here in recent years, however, and the campsites were closed for a while over safety concerns. It is therefore recommended to take local advice on the current situation before planning an overnight visit.) Mangatsiaka can be rewarding for Verreaux's sifakas, white-footed sportive lemurs and grey-brown mouse lemurs. Tsimelahy is worth visiting for its reptiles and unusual flora. The extreme heat can be tough-going.

MANDRARE VALLEY: BERENTY AND IFOTAKA

Berenty Private Reserve is one of the best-known sites in Madagascar, featured in numerous television documentaries. It is not pristine wilderness, nor is it comparable to other forest experiences in the country; it is a small island of natural habitat surrounded by a huge sisal plantation. Yet for many visitors it proves extremely rewarding with its combination of accessible accommodation, approachable lemurs and easy walking in the gallery forest. In adjacent areas of spiny bush, nocturnal mouse and sportive lemurs are readily seen, sometimes even during the day. This is one of the few reserves where visitors are permitted to wander without a guide, offering a rare opportunity to be alone with the wildlife. Berenty is the place to see Verreaux's sifakas 'dancing' across open ground and intimate encounters with troops of ring-tailed lemurs are guaranteed. There are equally friendly brown lemurs, hybrids of *Eulemur rufus* and *E. collaris*.

A short distance up the Mandrare Valley – just beyond the sisal plantation belt – is Ifotaka Community Forest, protecting primarily sub-arid thorn thicket with some dry gallery woodland. It was established in 2006 as the south's first protected area to involve local communities in its management. The traditional agricultural practice of land clearance (*hatsake*) by the agro-pastoral Antandroy people has posed serious problems, but sections of the forest are also highly valued as sacred areas – creating safe havens for lemur, bird and reptile populations to thrive in relatively intact spiny bush. The extensive species list is much the same as at Berenty, albeit far less habituated – but for some this is half of the appeal.

Habitat and Terrain

Berenty is situated on the west bank of the Mandrare River and is a small (265ha) isolated patch of gallery forest dominated by tamarind trees, some exceeding 20m. Adjacent are much smaller parcels of spiny bush dominated by *Alluaudia procera* and *A. ascendens*. The terrain is flat and walking is easy. North of Berenty, at Anjampolo, are more pristine parcels of spiny bush, dominated by various species of Didiereaceae including *Didierea madagascariensis*, *D. trolli*, *A. procera* and *A. ascendens*; Verreaux's sifakas and ring-tailed lemurs can be seen leaping among them.

Ring-tailed lemurs (see page 64) taking in the morning sun at Berenty. (CR)

In some parts of the main reserve an invasive vine (*Cissus quadrangularis*) is smothering and killing the forest and the habitat is becoming increasingly degraded. Ring-tailed lemurs feed on a toxic introduced tree, *Leucaena leucocephala*, causing some individuals to lose their fur in the dry season. Efforts are now being made to attempt to eradicate it.

Covering some 22,000ha, Ifotaka dwarfs Berenty, although many sections are sustainably managed rather than strictly protected, with certain areas set aside for cattle grazing and woodcutting for fuel.

Key Species

MAMMALS
Ring-tailed lemur, Verreaux's sifaka, grey mouse lemur, grey-brown mouse lemur, white-footed sportive lemur, brown lemurs (introduced at Berenty), lesser hedgehog tenrec, Madagascar flying fox and small Indian civet.

BIRDS
Giant coua, hook-billed vanga, ashy cuckoo shrike, Madagascar magpie-robin, Madagascar hoopoe, Madagascar paradise flycatcher, white-browed owl, Madagascar scops owl, Frances's sparrowhawk, Madagascar sparrowhawk, Madagascar harrier hawk, Madagascar cuckoo hawk and grey-headed lovebird.

REPTILES
Dumeril's boa, warty chameleon, jewel chameleon, radiated tortoise, spider tortoise, big-headed geckos (*Paroedura bastardi* and *P. picta*), plated lizard (*Zonosaurus trilineatus*) and a near-limbless lizard, *Androngo trivittatus*.

Visitor Information
Berenty is open year-round and is straightforward to reach: 3–4hrs west of Taolagnaro along a deteriorating road. April is the best month to see stink-fighting as the ring-tailed lemurs compete for mates. September and October are the prime months for baby lemurs, and reptiles are most active during and after the rains (Dec–Mar). There is an excellent network of wide paths and trails throughout the reserve. This is the only reserve suitable for wheelchairs or people with disabilities. Guides are available but not mandatory. Accommodation is in a complex of basic bungalows. Berenty is more expensive than other reserves but visitors will not be disappointed with the wildlife. A stay of one or two nights is recommended.

Those wishing to visit Ifotaka in comfort will find one of the country's finest lodges, with tented bungalows, located on the banks of the River Mandrare at the southern extremity of the protected area.

Mangrove estuary south of Belo-sur-Tsiribihina (NG/NHPA)

THREATENED WETLANDS

While pristine Madagascar centuries ago was covered in extensive forest, there were also natural wetland areas, both inland and around the coast, that harboured their own peculiar species. Some of these wetlands remain today, but until very recently they had largely been overlooked. Research by BirdLife International has shown that ten of the island's 15 endangered and critically endangered birds are predominantly wetland species. Also many lakes and rivers are home to a wealth of endemic fish, including some species popular in aquaria – but these are severely threatened by habitat degradation. Indeed, some are now extinct in the wild and survive only in aquaria.

Wetlands worldwide have been neglected as it is often assumed that there are more benefits for local people if they are drained and converted for agricultural use. This attitude has certainly prevailed in Madagascar, with its need to increase rice production, even though wetlands provide important fishing and hunting grounds and many other human benefits.

Mudskippers, which are related to gobies, are commonly seen in mangroves. They are able to remain out of water for several minutes to escape predators. While resting near the surface of the water their prominent eyes enable them to watch for danger both below and above water. (BL)

Important wetlands remain in the west, north and east. Some, like Lac Alaotra and the Lac Ihotry-Mangoky delta complex, are remote and far from established tourist circuits. Others, where visitor facilities are being improved, offer not only exciting wildlife-watching opportunities, but also the chance to experience relatively remote and untouched parts of the island.

BETSIBOKA DELTA

The Betsiboka is Madagascar's longest river, reaching the sea at Mahajanga on the northwest coast. Here its estuary is a wide single channel, but 15km inland is a complex of sandbars, mudflats, braided channels and mangroves that provide excellent habitats for many wetland birds, including a number of rare species.

Key Species
BIRDS
Madagascar teal and Madagascar sacred ibis (both sometimes in large numbers), Madagascar (Humblot's) heron, black egret, dimorphic egret and many other shore and wading birds.

Visitor Information
The best time for birding is September to December. Boat trips can be arranged through tour operators or hotels in Mahajanga.

LAC KINKONY AND THE MAHAVAVY DELTA

This area lies about 70km to the west of Mahajanga and is a complex of lakes, rivers, marshes, mangroves, deciduous forest and coastline covering almost 270,000ha. This includes Lac Kinkony, Madagascar's second largest lake. With such habitat variety, it is home to a wealth of wildlife, including at least ten species of lemur and

The Madagascar (or Humblot's) heron is a large, endemic heron best sought in the western wetlands such as the Betsiboka Delta. (NG)

over 140 bird species, many of which are regarded as threatened.

Key Species

MAMMALS
Decken's sifaka, mongoose lemur, red-fronted brown lemur, Ahmanson's sportive lemur and fat-tailed dwarf lemur.

BIRDS
Lac Kinkony is the only accessible site offering a chance to see the endangered Sakalava rail. The Mahavavy Delta is renowned for the Madagascar teal and Madagascar sacred ibis, as well as Madagascar (Humblot's) heron and Madagascar plover. Madagascar fish eagles may also be seen. Other threatened species: Madagascar grebe, Madagascar squacco (pond) heron, Madagascar pratincole and Madagascar plover.

Visitor Information
The best time for birding is the breeding season (Jul–Oct). Access is via the towns of Namakia and Mitsinjo. There are very limited facilities and conditions can be challenging. Excursions can be arranged through tour operators in Mahajanga or Antananarivo, working in conjunction with BirdLife International.

Birders exploring Lac Kinkony by boat (NG)

EMERGING THREATS: CHYTRID & INVASIVE TOADS

Amphibian chytrid fungus or 'Bd' is a microscopic parasite that can cause chytridiomycosis, a deadly disease in frogs. Spreading globally since its discovery in 1998, Bd has been implicated in countless population declines and extinctions, and by 2004 was estimated to have affected 30% of the world's 6,000 frog species.

The much-feared news that it had reached Madagascar came in March 2014. With such high amphibian diversity there, most species with localised distributions, the implications are very grave indeed. By testing swab samples taken from wild frogs, experts have confirmed the presence of Bd on the skins of multiple species at a number of sites across the country. However, at the time of writing, it has not yet been seen to cause any cases of chytridiomycosis. The reason for this is unknown; it is possible Malagasy frogs have an innate resistance or bacteria present on their skin keep Bd in check, or perhaps only less virulent Bd strains are so far present.

In any case, urgent preventative measures are now imperative. For your part, dry out any hiking or camping gear to prevent transfer of Bd between sites (it cannot survive more than 30mins without moist conditions) and if you see dead or dying frogs, note the location, take photos and report them via *www.sahonagasy.org*.

In a separate sinister development in March 2014, an influx of large exotic toads was detected around the city of Toamasina. The **Asian black-spined toad** (*Duttaphrynus melanostictus*) is widespread in south Asia and is very similar to the South American cane toad, which caused untold ecological damage after being introduced to Australia to control pests in 1935. It is not known how the black-spined toad reached Madagascar but it may have arrived as a cargo ship stowaway at Toamasina's large port. Some locals report first seeing the species in 2010 or 2011.

The black-spined toad could spread across the island wreaking environmental havoc: it's a hardy, highly adaptable species that breeds prolifically (a female can produce 40,000 eggs per clutch). Its toxic skin secretions pose a threat to native predators; even smaller predators may be poisoned by the eggs or tadpoles. The toad is voracious, feeding on insects, molluscs, centipedes, millipedes and scorpions as well as smaller frogs, reptiles and rodents. Even endemic species that would neither be consumed nor poisoned by the toads could still suffer from competition for resources with these invaders, or fall victim to foreign pathogens spread by them.

The adults can reach 20cm long and are of variable colour with a warty back and distinctive pronounced ridges on the head. They should not be handled but if you see one beyond the Toamasina region, report it to Sahonagasy. Urgent investigations are already under way to establish the feasibility of a necessary eradication programme.

Asian black-spined toad (DE)

MAMMALS

Ring-tailed lemur (NG)

Madagascar's mammals are unusual and enigmatic. One might expect them to be similar to those of nearby continental Africa, but that is far from the case. Madagascar has no herds of grazing animals, no large carnivores like cats or dogs, and no great apes or monkeys.

Smaller, less familiar creatures inhabit the island instead. In the forest canopies lemurs take the place of monkeys; carnivores are represented by such oddities as the fosa and mongoose-like carnivores; while bizarre tenrecs and peculiar rodents scuttle through the undergrowth. Only five major mammal groups have found their way here: bats, lemurs, rodents, tenrecs and mongoose-like carnivores.

The origin of Madagascar's mammals is a topic of great debate. Where did they come from? How did they get to the island? Which other mammals are their closest relatives? The application of new genetic techniques has greatly increased our understanding of the answers to these questions. Recently it has been discovered that the four main groups of terrestrial mammals – lemurs, rodents, tenrecs and carnivores – each originate from a single ancestor that colonised the island by chance millions of years ago.

LEMURS

The term 'lemur' was probably coined by early biologists as the calls of some species were reminiscent of the cries of *lemures* – spirits of the dead in Roman mythology.

Like us, lemurs are primates. They share some characteristics with early, ancestral primates, which the more advanced monkeys and apes subsequently lost.

Within the primates, lemurs belong to a group known as the Strepsirrhini suborder, which also includes the bushbabies (galagos) and pottos of Africa, and the lorises of southeast Asia. Unlike other strepsirrhine primates, many lemur species are diurnal and live in family groups or troops in which the females are dominant (this is unusual in primates: in most monkey and ape societies the males are socially dominant).

Another feature setting lemurs apart from their more intelligent monkey cousins is an acute sense of smell. Some species, particularly those more active during the day, have long, dog-like noses. Scents and smells are important in lemur society, being used extensively for communication, information-gathering and marking territorial boundaries.

By the time the earliest primates evolved, some 55mya, Madagascar had long broken away from Africa and arrived in its current position. The Mozambique Channel would have presented a formidable obstacle for any animal to cross. Some theories have suggested early primates (and other mammals) arrived via a series of now-submerged islands like stepping stones. But the weight of evidence is that lemur-like early primates arrived on floating rafts of vegetation washed out to sea from mainland Africa. The few unwitting mariners that survived this voyage provided the founding stock that has evolved into the wonderful variety of lemurs we see today.

Lemurs great and small. The indri (*left* AVZ) is the largest and most vocal living lemur. Madame Berthe's mouse lemur (*above* NG/NHPA) is probably the smallest primate in the world; it was described only in 2000.

Most predators – and all potential lemur competitors – missed the boat, so the early primate colonists had an uninhibited opportunity to diversify and exploit every available niche. Lemur diversity is impressive: all the recent splits and descriptions have resulted in more than 100 species (plus at least another 17 larger species have gone extinct since man's arrival). Today lemurs range in size from the tiny Madame Berthe's mouse lemur, which could sit comfortably in a small teacup, to the indri, a piebald teddy bear weighing in at almost 300 times as much. The extinct giant sloth lemurs of the genus *Archaeoindris* would have been 20 times heavier still, being similar in size to gorillas.

Biologists are fascinated by this great diversity (15 genera in five families); a third of the world's primate families occur only in Madagascar. To other visitors the appeal is more fundamental: lemurs are among the most cuddly, endearing and bewitching of creatures. Their soft fur, bright round eyes and gentle kid-gloved hands give them an irresistible appeal.

Leaves dominate the indri's diet; over 40 different species are eaten. (AVZ)

Indris can leap up to 10m between branches. (NG)

THE INDRI FAMILY

The indri family (Indriidae) comprises the indri, sifakas and woolly lemurs (avahis), totalling 19 species. All are strict vegetarians, mainly consuming leaves, buds, shoots, flowers and occasionally unripe fruits.

Indri

Indris live in the eastern rainforests in small family groups: normally an adult pair and their offspring. They pair for life, seeking a new partner only if their mate has died. Females give birth every other year to a single infant, so growth rates in indri populations are very slow. Indris announce their whereabouts with an eerie song that may carry for 2km; this serves as a warning to other groups to keep out of their territory. They are particularly vocal in the morning, typically engaging in three or four bouts of calling before noon. Males and females sometimes synchronise their calling, singing duets that may last three minutes. Besides singing, an average indri day consists of periods of feeding, followed by rest and sleep, before moving on to find more food.

Sifakas

There are nine species of sifaka (genus *Propithecus*), widely distributed across the island. Three are found in rainforest regions and six in dry forests. As well as being irresistibly cute, some are amongst the most colourful and distinctively marked of all lemurs, making them real favourites with visitors.

Coquerel's sifakas skipping across open ground. (DR)

The indri and sifakas have somewhat human proportions, with rather short arms and long, powerful legs. They are superb leapers and can jump effortlessly between trees many metres apart. But on the ground they are awkward. Visitors rarely see indri descend from the trees (except occasionally to eat soil), but sifakas inhabiting dry forest areas often cross open ground. They bound comically on their hind legs, providing visitors to places like Berenty with one of Madagascar's most memorable and amusing spectacles.

In the dry south and west, the sifakas are predominantly white (presumably to help control body temperature in this hot climate) with small patches of colour. Verreaux's sifaka (*Propithecus verreauxi*), white with a chocolate-coloured skullcap, is the most common and well known. It lives in the southern portion of the western deciduous forests and also throughout the spiny bush of the south, although it is patchily distributed because of habitat fragmentation. Verreaux's sifakas are one of the main attractions at the southern

Remarkably Verreaux's sifakas are able to leap and climb among the sharp-thorned boughs in the spiny bush without damaging their hands or feet. (NG/NPL)

reserves (Andohahela, Berenty, Isalo and Zombitse). It has a number of adaptations to living in such dry climates, including getting all the water it needs from the leaves it eats, rather than drinking.

Coquerel's sifaka (*P. coquereli*) is easily seen in the northwestern regions. Its chestnut-coloured arms and thighs, and piercing yellow eyes, make it particularly handsome. Like all sifakas, the young are born in June and July.

The two other species that inhabit western regions are harder to see as they live in more isolated areas. The crowned sifaka (*P. coronatus*) is white with a dark brown head and lives in a narrow area between the Betsiboka and Mahavavy rivers. And Decken's sifaka (*P. deckeni*) is completely white and is found in regions south of the Mahavavy River and north of the Manambolo River. It is most easily seen at Tsingy de Bemaraha.

In the eastern forests are found three species with distinct ranges. Many say the diademed sifaka (*P. diadema*) is the most beautiful of all lemurs: its silky coat is a combination of rich orange, gold, white, silver and black, and it has piercing ruby-red eyes. It is also the largest sifaka, weighing up to 6.5kg. Its range covers most of the northern half of the rainforest band.

Decken's sifaka from the west (NG/NPL)

Crowned sifaka (NG/NPL)

Diademed sifaka. At Mantadia some groups are habituated and can be approached, but they have large territories so may be difficult to find. Some have now been translocated back to the forest at Andasibe where they had died out in the 1960s due to human pressures. The distribution of the diademed sifaka is broadly similar to that of the indri. These two species share their habitat peacefully because they have very different diets, so they are not in competition for the same shoots and leaves. (NG)

Milne-Edwards' sifakas are frequently sighted at Ranomafana and also the private reserve of Ialatsara, 65km north of Fianarantsoa. (NG/NPL)

Relatively easily seen is Milne-Edwards' sifaka (*P. edwardsi*) of the central southeastern rainforest region. Its habitat has been fragmented severely and only a handful of larger forest areas remain where healthy populations are still found. At Ranomafana it has been studied for years, so groups are used to human presence. Studies have shown them to live in large ranges (up to 55ha), travel between 650m and 1,250m each day, and live up to 30 years.

Silky sifaka in Marojejy (NG)   Perrier's sifaka (NG/NPL)

The third and most endangered rainforest species is the pure white silky sifaka (*P. candidus*), which is restricted to the northern extremity of the rainforest band. Marojejy is the best place to look for this animal.

In the far northeastern corner of Madagascar, the two most critically endangered sifakas cling to survival. The hills around Daraina are the home of the golden-crowned sifaka (*P. tattersall*; see page 28). Forest clearance for agricultural and mining purposes has taken its toll on this species' habitat. A little further north, in the semi-humid forests of Analamera, lives the rarest of all: the jet-black Perrier's sifaka (*P. perrieri*). The total area of suitable forest habitat now measures just 20km by 20km, with probably fewer than 1,000 individuals remaining.

Woolly lemurs

Woolly lemurs (often simply called by their genus name, *Avahi*) are the only nocturnal members of the family, although they are often seen during the day sleeping in tangles of leaves or on branches. They may be mistaken for the similar-sized sportive lemurs although the distinctive white patches on the thighs of woolly lemurs are a characteristic feature. Woolly lemurs are relatively lethargic animals living on a low-energy diet of leaves. Even at night they spend much of their time resting, although in short bursts of activity they can leap speedily through the forest canopy.

After recent additions to the scientific register, nine species are now known. The eastern woolly lemur (*Avahi laniger*) is found throughout much of the eastern rainforest band. The others have much more restricted ranges: the western woolly lemur (*A. occidentalis*) around Ankarafantsika, the Sambirano woolly lemur (*A. unicolor*) from the Sambirano region in the northwest, Cleese's woolly lemur (*A. cleesei*) at Bemaraha, Moore's woolly lemur (*A. mooreorum*) in Masoala, the Betsileo woolly lemur (*A. betsileo*) at Fandriana, Peyrieras' woolly lemur (*A. peyrierasi*) in Ranomafana, Ramanantsoavana's woolly lemur (*A. ramanantsoavana*) at Manombo, and the southern woolly lemur (*A. meridionalis*) around Andohahela.

Eastern woolly lemurs are easily seen at Andasibe-Mantadia and Ranomafana. (NG)

Western woolly lemur. Ankarafantsika is the best place to see this species. (NG)

TRUE LEMURS

The true lemurs (family Lemuridae) are the most familiar lemurs, regularly encountered in the majority of protected areas, as well as in zoos. All are skilled climbers and spend varying amounts of time on the ground.

Ring-tailed lemur

Most captivating is surely the iconic national animal, the ring-tailed lemur (*Lemur catta*), which has become synonymous with Madagascar. Yet they are not typical; ring-tails spend more time on the ground than other lemurs and form the largest social groups, sometimes with 20 or more individuals. In this female-dominated society scent plays an essential role in establishing hierarchy and communication. They may often be observed scent-marking by rubbing their anal glands against trees; males also use a spur and gland on their wrists to gouge tree bark as a visible 'keep out' sign for rival troops. During the breeding season (mid-April to mid-May) males also indulge in stink fights. After anointing their tails with scent from their wrist glands, they face one another and waft their quivering tails towards their opponents like smelly black-and-white flags.

Unusually for true lemurs, ring-
tails often have twins. (HB)

Ring-tails are highly vocal and have a repertoire of calls: some warn of danger (with different calls for aerial and terrestrial predators), while their early-morning call is like the mewing of a cat (hence the name *catta*).

Their varied diet ranges from fruit, leaves, flowers, bark and sap to the occasional insect and small reptile. Unlike the Verreaux's sifakas which share their range, they need to drink, so are more sparsely distributed in the arid spiny bush compared to deciduous and gallery forests, where water sources are more readily available.

Ring-tailed lemurs have a broad range throughout the south and southwest of Madagascar. There is even an isolated population high in the Andringitra Massif among the heathers and sub-alpine vegetation. These animals, which have been observed at elevations up to 2,600m, have thicker coats to protect against cold and sometimes sleep in caves at night.

A ring-tail scenting its tail in preparation for stink fighting. Berenty remains the easiest place to see them, but they can also be encountered at Isalo, Andringitra, Tsimanampetsotsa and Anja. (CR)

Typical lemurs (genus *Eulemur*)

Widespread throughout all forests of Madagascar except the spiny bush, the *Eulemur* species share several characteristics. Almost all are sexually dichromatic: males are differently marked and coloured from females. Scent also plays an important part in marking territories; females generally spray urine, while males smear secretions from their anal region or heads onto strategic objects – which may include females.

For a long time these lemurs were thought to be primarily diurnal, but research has revealed that all species can also be active at night, the extent of which depends on the lunar cycle (they are more active during full moon), food availability and season. Species with both diurnal and nocturnal habits are referred to as cathemeral.

There are eleven species of *Eulemur*. The rare mongoose lemur (*Eulemur mongoz*) can sometimes be seen at Ankarafantsika. Its behaviour changes with the seasons. During the warm wet months (December to April) they tend to be more active during the day, but from the dry season in May there is a marked shift towards nocturnal activity. This strategy may help them conserve energy when food is less plentiful as well as reducing the chance of predation by birds of prey when there is little protective foliage on the trees.

Red-bellied lemur. Males have distinctive white 'tear-drop' marks beneath their eyes. (HB)

The red-bellied lemur (*E. rubriventer*) is found throughout the eastern rainforests and is unusual in that it lives in monogamous pairs rather than large troops. Both sexes take their parental responsibilities seriously and carry the infants on their backs, but the males tend to take over more as the youngsters become heavier.

They are a rich chestnut colour, but only the male has the red belly that gives them their name; the female's is creamy-white.

Crowned lemurs (*E. coronatus*) are found only in the far north. The male's orange-brown coat, ginger ruff and crown, and black head stripe contrast strongly with the grey females and their ginger tiaras.

Male crowned lemur (see page 27 for female). This species is easy to see at Montagne d'Ambre and Ankarana. (NG)

The black lemur (*E. macaco*) and the blue-eyed black lemur (*E. flavifrons*) are only found in the northwest, mainly in isolated areas. These are the most extremely sexually dichromatic of all lemurs. So different are males from females that it would be easy to think they are separate species. The difference in colour between the sexes is more pronounced in the black lemur: males are all black with bright orange eyes, while females are chestnut brown with white ear tufts. The blue-eyed black lemur is critically endangered and lives only on the Sahamalaza Peninsula opposite Nosy Be. The forests here are extremely fragmented and this species' survival hangs in the balance. Interestingly it is the only non-human primate to have blue eyes.

Black lemurs (male *left*, and female, *right*). These are most readily seen at Lokobe on Nosy Be and on nearby Nosy Komba, where they have become very tame. (*both* AVZ)

Female blue-eyed black lemur; the Sahamalaza Peninsula, where this species lives, is one of Madagascar's newest national parks – see page 30. (NG)

Common brown lemur. Although hardly 'common' it is readily seen at Ankarafantsika and Andasibe. Unlike other *Eulemur* species, the two sexes are very similar in appearance. (NG)

BROWN LEMURS

With recent revisions in classification, seven species of brown lemur are now recognised. The females of all species are largely uniform in colour and similar to one another, generally with a brown body and black or grey head. It is the handsome males that show off with a variety of markings, colours and facial hair tufts, setting themselves apart from their mates and from males of the other species.

The various brown lemur species inhabit distinct ranges, which collectively form a broad ring around Madagascar's periphery, although because of forest fragmentation it is no longer continuous.

White-fronted brown lemur. The male, with his white head and creamy underparts, is gorgeous; the female is less impressive. (KF)

The distributions of both the common and red-fronted brown lemurs (*E. fulvus* and *E. rufifrons*) are interesting as each species' range straddles both rainforest and dry deciduous forests areas. Most likely, when forest cover was more extensive, these lemurs also inhabited the connecting areas across the now barren central highlands.

The white-fronted brown lemur (*E. albifrons*) and Sanford's brown lemur (*E. sanfordi*; see page 11) are both notable for their splendid white whiskers. Although both occur in northern Madagascar, their ranges do not overlap so there is little chance of confusion.

In rufous and red-fronted brown lemurs (*E. rufus and E. rufifrons*), males have a greyish-brown coat with a distinctive rusty crown, while females tend to be paler chestnut brown. Both sexes have conspicuous white patches above their eyes, most defined in females. In rainforest areas like Ranomafana, the body colour of red-fronted brown lemurs tends to be darker than that of their counterparts in dry deciduous forests such as Kirindy.

Brown lemurs generally live in troops of between five and 15 animals with roughly equal numbers of males and females. Most prefer fruit as the mainstay of their diet, augmented by leaves and flowers. In Ranomafana, red-fronted brown lemurs have been observed eating giant millipedes, first wiping off any unpleasant secretions with its tail, before tucking into this unlikely snack.

A male red-fronted brown lemur. There are noticeable differences in colouration across this species' range, especially between east and west. Females tend to be browner and lack the male's rusty crown. (NG)

Ruffed lemurs

Ruffed lemurs (genus *Varecia*) are the largest and arguably most impressive members of the Lemuridae family. The two recognised species, black-and-white ruffed lemur (*V. variegata*) and red ruffed lemur (*V. rubra*), are confined to eastern rainforests, but their ranges do not overlap. There are three subspecies of black-and-white ruffed lemur.

Fruit is the mainstay of their diet and their territories are always centred on the largest fruiting trees. Such trees are often first to be removed when forest is cleared, making ruffed lemurs particularly susceptible to habitat disturbance. In addition their large size (with plenty of meat) and luxuriant fur means they are prime targets for hunters. Consequently, both species have become very rare and are now seriously threatened. Ironically they adapt well to captivity, so are among the species most regularly seen in zoos. In 2001, there were some 660 in European zoos alone – all descended from 28 founding animals.

Black-and-white ruffed lemurs (*left* DA) are now very patchily distributed over the northern, central and southeastern rainforests. They can sometimes be seen at Ranomafana or Mantadia, and more easily on Nosy Mangabe where they were introduced over 40 years ago. The red ruffed lemur (*right* NG/NPL) is confined to the Masoala Peninsula. The Antainambalana River forms a natural barrier separating this species from its black-and-white cousin. Both species can be extremely vocal and have loud raucous calls.

Unusually, both species generally produce twins or sometimes triplets and these are born in September and October. Unlike other infant lemurs, baby ruffed lemurs do not cling to their mothers but are parked in a nest while she forages. If the young need to be moved, she carries them in her mouth.

Bamboo lemurs

The bamboo lemurs are a distinctive group within the Lemuridae family, although they show some close affinities to the ring-tailed lemur. These endearing animals are Madagascar's miniature equivalents of giant pandas, bamboo and similar plants making up most of their diet. After recent amendments to taxonomy, six species are now recognised; five in the genus *Hapalemur* (weighing 750–1,600g) and a single species, the greater bamboo lemur, in the genus *Prolemur*.

The most widespread is the grey bamboo lemur (*H. griseus*), now divided into three subspecies. The nominate subspecies *H. g. griseus* is found in central eastern rainforest regions and is most easily seen in Andasibe-Mantadia, often close to roads or tracks where forest edge vegetation is dominated by bamboo species.

The second subspecies, the Ranomafana bamboo lemur (*H. g. ranomafanensis*), is found in rainforest areas centred on the eponymous national park, but interestingly also in remote parts of western madagascar, like Bemaraha. Presumably this distribution would once have been continuous when forests of the central highlands were intact. The final subspecies, *H. g. gilberti*, is only known from a restricted locality in the central eastern region near Beanamalao.

The greater bamboo lemur feeds almost exclusively on giant bamboo. To avoid competition with golden bamboo lemurs, which mainly eat the shoots and young leaves of these plants, they prefer the inner pith. The damage caused by their strong jaws and large teeth in stripping away the outer layers of bamboo is clear evidence of this species' presence. (NG/NPL)

Eastern grey bamboo lemur. While feeding principally on bamboo, this species also eats other foliage, grasses, flowers and occasionally fungi. (DA)

Other *Hapalemur* species are also challenging to see as they live in less accessible locations. At the southern extreme of the rainforest belt lives the southern bamboo lemur (*H. meridionalis*) that may be seen at Andohahela or Mandena. The northern bamboo lemur (*H. occidentalis*) can be encountered in Marojejy and forests of the Sambirano region.

The Lac Alaotra reed lemur (*H. alaotrensis*) is extremely specialised and is unique amongst primates in that it lives most of its life in reed and papyrus beds above water. As a major rice-growing centre, the lake is being drained and cleared. These activities have caused a catastrophic decline in its lemur population – perhaps as few as 2,500 to 5,000 survive.

At least as endangered is the golden bamboo lemur (*H. aureus*) which was not discovered until 1985 and became the catalyst for the creation of Ranomafana National Park. It was subsequently also found at Andringitra and the forest corridor connecting the two areas, but perhaps fewer than 2,000 individuals remain.

Golden bamboo lemurs are rich golden-brown, especially their underparts, limbs and face. They are principally diurnal and have a particular preference for the young leaves and new shoots of giant bamboo which, while rich in protein, also contain high levels of cyanide that would be lethal to other animals. This species is generally seen in family groups of two to six, but three or four is normal.

The greater bamboo lemur (*Prolemur simus*) is the largest of the bamboo lemurs: at 2–2½kg, it is twice the weight of the others. Subfossils show this lemur was once widespread in rainforest areas, but its range has become far more restricted with forest fragmentation. Until very recently it was thought only to survive in Ranomafana, Andringitra and Kianjavato, but new research has revealed some encouraging surprises. Small isolated populations have now been found near Mantadia and further north and east. Many of these sites are degraded, but ironically these lemurs may benefit as the giant bamboo they rely on flourishes under such conditions.

MOUSE LEMURS AND DWARF LEMURS

This family (Cheirogaleidae) contains at least 33 species. They range between very small and medium-small with long tails, short legs, a mainly horizontal body posture, and they run and jump using all fours.

The grey mouse lemur is one of the largest *Microcebus* species and is easily seen in Kirindy and Ankarafantsika. (NG)

Mouse lemurs

The diminutive, animated mouse lemurs (genus *Microcebus*) are the smallest and most abundant primates in Madagascar. Currently 21 species are recognised, ranging in weight from around 30g to 75g (it varies significantly with season). Many of them are so similar in appearance that distinguishing them in the field is difficult.

The old school of thought suggested the grey mouse lemur (*M. murinus*) lived in the drier forests of the west, while the brown mouse lemur (*M. rufus*) inhabited the wetter east. In all regions, so many new species have now been described that it is impossible to be precise on distributions and how species relate to established forms; a considerable amount of research needs to be done.

Madame Berthe's mouse lemur (*M. berthae*) is the world's smallest primate, weighing a mere 25–35g. It is only known from the dry forest areas of Menabe; Kirindy is the best place to see it. Being so minute, mouse lemurs have correspondingly small home ranges – typically covering around 1ha.

Goodman's mouse lemur was described in 2005 from the Forêt d'Analamazaotra near Andasibe. (NG)

Other well-established species include the golden-brown mouse lemur (*M. ravelobensis*) from Ankarafantsika, the grey-brown mouse lemur (*M. griseorufus*) from southern spiny bush areas (including Berenty and the Arboretum d'Antsokay near Toliara), and the northern rufous mouse lemur (*M. tavaratra*) from the Ankarana area. In addition, in eastern rainforests several new species have been named after eminent scientists: Goodman's mouse lemur (*M. lehilahytsara*), Jolly's mouse lemur (*M. jollyae*), Simmons' mouse lemur (*M. simmonsi*) and Mittermeier's mouse lemur (*M. mittermeieri*). There have been other species recently described, some still only known from the original location.

Dwarf lemurs

Recent taxonomical changes have also greatly affected the dwarf lemurs (genus *Cheirogaleus*). There are two well-documented species: the greater dwarf lemur (*Cheirogaleus major*) in the east and the fat-tailed dwarf lemur (*C. medius*; see page 165) in the west. Extensive work is underway to verify the distributions and validity of the new species.

Greater dwarf lemur in Marojejy (NG)

Most easily seen is the furry-eared dwarf lemur (*C. crossleyi*), which, in the warm season (October to May), is commonly encountered along the roadside near Andasibe. During the cooler winter months dwarf lemurs aestivate, living off fat reserves built up in their tails during the times of summer plenty – a unique feature among primates (the tail can account for 40% of their body weight).

Furry-eared dwarf lemur at Andasibe (NG)

Because it lives in the more seasonal forests of the west, the fat-tailed dwarf lemur's activity periods are governed by local conditions. In particularly cool, dry years it may be inactive for several months during the winter. But even when active they are much slower-moving than the scampering mouse lemurs.

Other cheirogaleids

The remaining members of the family include two giant dwarf (or giant mouse) lemurs: *Mirza coquereli* and *M. zaza*. They are more omnivorous than other lemurs, with insects and other invertebrates forming a large part of their diet.

There are at least four species of fork-marked lemur (genus *Phaner*), all with a characteristic black dorsal line that splits into two on the crown with each branch ending at an eye. They are primarily canopy dwellers so are challenging to see well – although, being very vocal, they are often heard.

The hairy-eared dwarf lemur (*Allocebus trichotis*) led biologists on a merry dance for many years. Originally known from just five museum specimens, it was not rediscovered until 1989. For some time thereafter, its range was believed to be restricted to lowland rainforests near Mananara, but sightings in the past decade have confirmed other localities throughout the northern half of the rainforest band.

Once considered critically endangered, it turns out that the hairy-eared dwarf lemur is not so rare after all. It can even be seen around Andasibe and Mantadia, especially in the Forêt d'Analamazaotra administered by Association Mitsinjo. (NG)

SPORTIVE (OR WEASEL) LEMURS

Sportive lemurs (family Lepilemuridae) are often referred to by their genus name, *Lepilemur*. More than any other, the scientific classification of this group has been turned on its head by a recent explosion in the descriptions of new species. For the most part these descriptions are based on genetic differences rather than outwardly visible features, making recognition of species in the field very difficult. The ranges of the 26 species now described together form a discontinuous ring around Madagascar. These ranges do not overlap, so geographical location is the most reliable means of sportive lemur identification.

Sportive lemurs are medium-sized with long tails. Although nocturnal, they are most often seen during the day peering dozily out of their tree holes or from concealed forks in branches. At night, they can be very vocal and active, their powerful hind legs enabling them to leap impressive distances in search of food – normally leaves and small flowers.

Red-tailed sportive lemur (*Lepilemur ruficaudatus*) in Kirindy (NG/NHPA)

Ankarana sportive lemur (*Lepilemur ankaranensis*) is found only in forests in the extreme north of the island. (NG/NHPA)

Hubbard's sportive lemur (*Lepilemur hubbardi*) was recently described from Zombitse. (DA)

Aye-aye (NG)

AYE-AYE

Perhaps more than any other mammal, the aye-aye (*Daubentonia madagascariensis*) epitomises all that is bizarre and compelling about Madagascar's wildlife. It is a seriously weird animal that scientists originally classified as a squirrel. So unique is this species that it is not only the sole living member of its genus, but also of its family (Daubentoniidae).

What makes it so unusual? It has a disproportionately long and bushy tail; incisor teeth like a rodent's that never stop growing; ears resembling large radar dishes that are so sensitive they can detect a grub moving under the bark of a tree; claws rather than fingernails (except on the great toe); inguinal teats (between its back legs not on its chest); no fixed mating season; and its celebrated extraordinary middle finger.

Often described as 'greatly elongated', this finger is in fact no longer proportionally than in other primates (including man). But it is extraordinarily thin – skeletally so, for it has no flesh – adding to the illusion of extra length. The aye-aye keeps its other fingers crooked up out of the way when working with its most important digit, so its hand looks like a tarantula. The slender finger is like a built-in Swiss Army knife, designed to fit through gnawed holes in trees or nuts (coconuts are a favourite) to winkle out the tasty contents. All the time its ears swivel, listening for the slightest sound.

It is no surprise, then, that the aye-aye is a focus of Malagasy folklore and superstition – much of it contradictory. Local taboos (*fady*) differ across the country and may even be exclusive to a single village. Most regard the aye-aye as an omen of evil, sickness or death; some in the far north even say that aye-ayes eat people! And so in many areas the aye-aye is persecuted and killed in an attempt to dispel any evil spirits. Yet others believe aye-ayes to be the reincarnated spirits of their ancestors, and so bestow upon them the highest of honours usually reserved for important chiefs.

It was long believed that the aye-aye was close to extinction. However, in recent years it has become apparent that they are actually the most widely distributed lemur species. It is not that their population has made an astonishing recovery, but simply that our knowledge of these creatures has improved. Nevertheless, sighting a wild aye-aye is a very rare event; not only are their territories huge and their population density low, but they move high in the forest canopy under the cover of darkness.

An aye-aye putting its specially adapted finger to use winkling out grubs. Uniquely this digit articulates through a ball-and-socket joint, allowing it to swivel in a full circle. (NG)

MALAGASY CARNIVORES
UNRAVELLING CARNIVORE CONFUSION

Madagascar's endemic carnivores, of which there are 11 species, have long been the subject of heated debate among biologists. Because of their variety in size and shape, and the apparent lack of close relatives elsewhere in the world (particularly mainland Africa), their origin has proved to be something of an enigma.

Three of the genera (*Cryptoprocta, Fossa* and *Eupleres*) were long thought to be allied to civets (family Viverridae), while the other seven species (in the genera *Galidia, Galidictis, Mungotictis* and *Salanoia*) were considered relatives of the mongooses (family Herpestidae). However, the latest genetic research provides compelling evidence that all these species evolved from a single common ancestor that was closely related neither to the civets nor to the mongooses, making the Malagasy carnivores an ancient lineage with no close living relatives. Consequently they have now been classified in their own separate family, Eupleridae.

A great deal of inconsistency exists over their English common names, with terms like 'civet' and 'mongoose' now rendered inappropriate because they imply incorrect evolutionary relationships. In addition, most species have multiple common names derived from regional Malagasy terms or now spurious English names, fuelling the confusion. Further, recent research has split some species into two distinct ones, with each then requiring precise naming to prevent ambiguity. To remove confusion, there is now a concerted effort to shift to a standardised set of common names as follows.

New Name	Scientific Name	Obsolete Name
fosa	*Cryptoprocta ferox*	fossa
eastern falanouc	*Eupleres goudotii*	falanouc
western falanouc	*Eupleres major*	falanouc
spotted fanaloka	*Fossa fossana*	Malagasy civet or fanaloka
ring-tailed vontsira	*Galidia elegans*	ring-tailed mongoose
broad-striped vontsira	*Galidictis fasciata*	broad-striped mongoose
Grandidier's vontsira	*Galidictis grandidieri*	Grandidier's mongoose
northern bokiboky	*Mungotictis decemlineata*	narrow-striped mongoose
southern bokiboky	*Mungotictis lineata*	narrow-striped mongoose
brown-tailed vontsira	*Salanoia concolor*	brown-tailed mongoose
Durrell's vontsira	*Salanoia durrelli*	Durrell's brown-tailed mongoose

THE LARGER CARNIVORES

The fosa (*Cryptoprocta ferox*) is Madagascar's largest carnivore, measuring up to 1.7m long – half of which is tail used for balance when climbing. It vaguely resembles an elongated, short-legged puma (when first discovered it was thought to be a type of cat), although its general build is more slender and it generally weighs no more than 10kg (males).

Fosas are usually nocturnal, secretive and solitary; but in the mating season (October to December) they can lose their shyness and are famously promiscuous.

A female in oestrous climbs a favoured mating tree and may attract the attention of up to ten males simultaneously, who then vie for her affections in turn. Copulation, which is often noisy, may last from several minutes to as long as six hours, and during her period of fertility a female can mate as many as 50 times, spending up to 40 hours in total in the act! Such extreme competition has led males to evolve disproportionately large penises, presumably as a means of implanting the copious quantities of semen they produce more deeply into the female; the deeper it is implanted, the better chance it has in beating the competing males' sperm in the race to fertilise the egg.

An outstanding climber, the fosa is equally at home in the trees and on the ground. Lemurs are their main prey, although they will feed on all manner of other animals. This is a rare sighting of one in the rainforest canopy, although Kirindy in the west remains the best place to see them. (NG)

Spotted fanaloka. In preparation for the leaner winter months, this species is able to lay down fat reserves, especially in its tail; this may constitute 25% of the animal's body weight. (NG/NHPA)

The secretive spotted fanaloka (*Fossa fossana*) is a small carnivore about the size of a domestic cat. They live in pairs in the eastern rainforests and deciduous forests of the far north, foraging for food in the dense undergrowth. A pair marks their territory (about 50ha) with scent from glands around the anus, cheeks and neck.

Madagascar's most specialised carnivore is the falanouc (genus *Eupleres*), now recognised as two species: the eastern falanouc (*E. goudotii*) and the western falanouc (*E. major*). These uncommon and secretive fox-like animals prefer marshy areas. The eastern falanouc lives in the rainforest regions, while the western one is associated with swampy areas of dry forests in the northwest.

Both species of falanouc are noticeably larger than the spotted fanaloka and have an extended pointy snout, small teeth and forepaws with strong claws for digging – features that help them forage for earthworms, their main food. They give birth to extremely well-developed young; the babies are born with their eyes open and are able to follow their mother and hide in vegetation within two days.

The ring-tailed vontsira is most easily seen at Ranomafana and Marojejy (eastern subspecies) or Montagne d'Ambre and Ankarana (northern subspecies). (NG)

THE SMALLER CARNIVORES

The most common and widespread species is the ring-tailed vontsira (*Galidia elegans*), of which there are three subspecies, each inhabiting different forest regions, in the east, north and west. They are diurnal with a rich russet coat and distinctive banded tail. These sociable creatures, often found in vocal family groups, are equally at home on the ground or in the branches of trees, foraging for eggs, young birds, rodents, reptiles and invertebrates.

Two species are now recognised in the genus *Mungotictis*, the northern bokiboky (*M. decemlineata*) and the southern bokiboky (*M. lineata*). They are found in the drier regions between the Fiherenana River north of Toliara and the Tsiribihina River north of Kirindy. The northern and southern species are separated by the Mangoky River. These delightful sandy-grey animals have several faint stripes along their flanks and back, and a large bushy tail, which they hold erect when alarmed. Foraging over large areas, they can cover 2km in a day. Their diet is dominated by insects, particularly grubs and larvae excavated from rotting wood.

The northern bokiboky is social, living in family units, preferring areas of forest with dense undergrowth.
(NG/NPL)

The genus *Galidictis* comprises two little-known species. In the rainforest regions lives the broad-striped vontsira (*G. fasciata*), a very distinctive but enigmatic carnivore that is known to be strictly nocturnal but is hardly ever seen. Grandidier's vontsira (*G. grandidieri*) was not described until 1986 and is noticeably larger than its congener. The species is restricted to the spiny bush on the eastern side of Lac Tsimanampetsotsa. It is also strictly nocturnal and feeds mainly on invertebrates, including hissing cockroaches and scorpions.

Equally mysterious are the two species of *Salanoia*. The brown-tailed vontsira (*S. concolor*) is known only from the northern rainforests. It is diurnal and mainly terrestrial, feeding mostly on insects. Betampona is the only place where it is seen with any regularity. Recently described is Durrell's vontsira (*S. durrelli*), found only in the reed beds around Lac Alaotra and named in recognition of Gerald Durrell, who did so much to champion Madagascar's endangered wildlife.

TENRECS

Tenrecs (family Tenrecidae) are early offshoots from the evolutionary line that gave rise to the insectivores. Like all of the island's terrestrial mammal groups, it is now known they evolved from a single common ancestor. Since this initial colonisation they have diversified spectacularly to fill numerous small mammal niches. These

include parallels with hedgehogs, moles, desmans, otter-shrews, true shrews and even small tree-dwelling mice. An incredible diversity of tenrecs may share a single habitat: some eastern rainforests are known to support as many as 17 different species in the same area.

At least 30 species of these nocturnal creatures have been described thus far, and new ones are still being discovered. Tenrecs are divided into two sub-families: the five spiny tenrecs (Tenrecinae) and 25 or so furred tenrecs (Oryzorictinae). During, the cooler winter months when food is scarce, many become inactive.

Not all the spiny tenrecs live up to their name. The largest, the common (or tailless) tenrec (*Tenrec ecaudatus*), has only a few spines hidden in its coarse fur. It is widespread, even outside forest areas, and weighs up to 2kg, making it a popular source of

Common tenrecs have voracious appetites and use their powerful snouts to search for insects, grubs and other invertebrates. (AVZ)

bushmeat for the rural Malagasy.

Their reproductive capabilities are remarkable: they can produce up to 32 offspring in one litter (typically 20–5 in the wild) and have 17 pairs of nipples – the mammalian record. Not all the babies survive, but those that do emerge from their nest at around 20 days old and follow their mother around the forest in orderly columns, wearing stripy, spiny coats for camouflage and defence. They begin to

become independent after 35 days and their juvenile streaks disappear at two months.

The greater and lesser hedgehog tenrecs (*Setifer setosus* and *Echinops telfairi*) look very much like hedgehogs, rolling themselves into prickly balls when disturbed. The former is found in both western and eastern forests, while the latter is restricted to the drier regions of the southwest.

In rainforest areas, the most commonly encountered species are the highland and lowland streaked tenrecs (*Hemicentetes nigriceps* and *H. semispinosus*). Both have sharp yellow spines mixed with softer black prickles arranged in stripes, and orange-yellow underparts. A specialised set of spines on the back of the neck is used for

Despite their rotund appearance, lesser hedgehog tenrecs are surprisingly agile and capable of climbing along thin twigs using their short tail as a brace. (NG)

communication; they can be vibrated to produce a threatening rattle (called stridulation) or a sound to call straying youngsters and other family members, which is inaudible to humans.

The furred tenrecs have evolved to fill niches occupied elsewhere by shrews, moles, desmans and arboreal mice. Most are shrew tenrecs (genus *Microgale*), which

Highland (*left* DA) and lowland (*right* NG) streaked tenrecs. Although principally nocturnal, they are sometimes active and encountered during the day. Andasibe-Mantadia, Ranomafana and Marojejy are good places to see the lowland species while the highland one may be found in Andringitra.

range in size from the tiny pygmy shrew tenrec (*Microgale parvula*) – weighing just 3g – to the carnivorous Talazac's shrew tenrec (*M. talazaci*), which weighs up to 40g. The lesser long-tailed shrew tenrec (*M. longicaudata*) has an outrageously long tail (more than twice its body length) that is prehensile, helping it to climb. The majority of shrew tenrecs appear very similar and can sometimes only be distinguished by close expert examination.

Superficially similar to the shrew tenrecs is the large-eared tenrec (*Geogale aurita*). This has some very primitive characteristics and may have been amongst the first tenrecs to evolve. They inhabit western and southwestern forests and use their keen hearing to locate ants and termites in rotting wood.

Mole tenrecs (genus *Oryzorictes*) are rather stocky with soft, velvety fur. Like moles, they have very strong forelimbs, large spade-like front feet and very small eyes and ears – all adaptations to burrowing. Because of their subterranean way of life they are hardly ever seen.

The largest and most specialised member of this subfamily is the remarkable aquatic tenrec (*Limnogale mergulus*), which has developed webbed feet and a flattened tail for swimming. It lives in fast-flowing streams where it forages for aquatic insect larvae and crustaceans (a similar lifestyle to desmans and otter-shrews elsewhere). During the day it sleeps in a streamside burrow, only emerging to forage after dark. While the animal itself is rarely seen, it leaves conspicuous evidence of its presence in the form of latrine sites on prominent boulders or fallen trees in mid-stream.

RODENTS

Madagascar's native rodents are diverse in size, form and lifestyle. But despite this great variety, genetic techniques have shown that the 24 recognised species all evolved from one common ancestor that colonised the island millions of years ago.

All native species belong to the endemic subfamily Nesomyinae, which contains nine genera. Their diversity in appearance is startling, with some similar to that are gerbils (*Macrotarsomys*), voles (*Brachyuromys*), arboreal mice (*Eliurus*), and even rabbits (*Hypogeomys*).

The island's most celebrated rodent is the nocturnal giant jumping rat (*Hypogeomys antimena*; see page 35) which is found only in a tiny area in the west (no more than 800km²) centred on Kirindy. This charming animal is the size of a rabbit and fills a similar ecological niche. It excavates extensive burrows, so it is restricted to areas with sandy soils and dry leaf litter. Their burrows normally lie at the heart of a 3–4ha territory.

The giant jumping rat's name derives from its kangaroo-like method of locomotion when alarmed. Most unusually for a rodent, this species is monogamous, with pair bonds generally lasting until the death of one partner.

Perhaps the most readily seen native rodents are the eastern and lowland red forest rats (*Nesomys rufus* and *N. audeberti*), both of which are diurnal (unusual for tropical rodents) and common in many rainforests, including Ranomafana and Andasibe-Mantadia.

In Ranomafana the red forest rat is often seen foraging amongst fallen branches and leaf litter, and is sometimes extremely confiding. (NG/NPL)

Nocturnal white-tailed tree rats (genus *Brachytarsomys*), of which there are two species, also inhabit rainforest areas and are unusual in that they are totally arboreal. They have developed extremely short, broad feet and long, flexible tails to act as a counterbalance when climbing.

The ten tuft-tailed rats (genus *Eliurus*) are also nocturnal and arboreal, and generally occur in rainforests. They sport tails with conspicuous brush-like tufted ends of varying degrees of bushiness. The tails are 15–30% longer than the body.

Webb's tuft-tailed rat (*Eliurus webbi*) (DA)

The smallest rodents are the three species of big-footed mice (genus *Macrotarsomys*), which are confined to the drier forests and grasslands of the west. Most easily seen is the western big-footed mouse (*Macrotarsomys bastardi*), often encountered on night walks in Kirindy and Ankarafantsika. The long-tailed big-footed mouse (*M. ingens*), endemic to the Ankarafantsika area, is particularly impressive.

Other endemic rodents include: the vole rats (genus *Brachyuromys*) that construct networks of runways beneath thick tangles of vegetation and matted grasses; the *voalavo* (*Voalavo gymnocaudus*), a diminutive species recently described from high montane forests in the northeast; the *voalavoanala* (*Gymnuromys roberti*), a species that has remained rather mysterious ever since its discovery in 1896; and the Malagasy mountain mouse (*Monticolomys koopmani*), another recent addition to the scientific register that is known only from higher elevations.

The tail of the long-tailed big-footed mouse can be 24cm long – nearly double its body length. (NG)

BATS

Bats (order Chiroptera) are split into two distinct groups: the fruit bats and flying foxes (suborder Megachiroptera), and the insectivorous-type bats (suborder Microchiroptera). Both are represented in Madagascar.

Given the relative ease with which bats can travel over long distances (and more importantly over water) it is hardly surprising that there are proportionally fewer endemic species, compared to other mammal groups in Madagascar. Even so, at least 70% of the bats are endemic.

There are three species of fruit bat, the largest being the Madagascar flying fox (*Pteropus rufus*), with a wingspan up to 1.5m and weight of 1kg or more. The name flying fox is appropriate; they do indeed look like little foxes with their long muzzles and pointed ears. They are proficient fliers – covering up to 50km (30 miles) in a night – and roost in large colonies, generally in remote forests or on islands around the coast where the levels of disturbance are low.

Madagascar flying fox (NG/NPL)

The next-largest species is the straw-coloured fruit bat (*Eidolon dupreanum*), which is widespread but patchily distributed. It roosts in colonies of up to 500 in large trees, on cliffs or in buildings, and is the only fruit bat known to occur on the high plateau.

The Madagascar rousette (*Rousettus madagascariensis*) is found both in rainforests and in deciduous forests. It prefers to roost deep in caves, rather than in trees, and has some rudimentary echolocation capabilities to aid orientation in low light. Large cave systems, such as those at Ankarana, may be inhabited by colonies of several thousand individuals.

Straw-coloured fruit bats (PC)

Seven families from the suborder Microchiroptera are represented in Madagascar, although only one of these, Myzopodidae, is endemic. It contains the two species of sucker-footed bat (genus *Myzopoda*), which derive their name from the peculiar suction discs on their wrists and feet that help them to hang from smooth

leaves like palms. The eastern sucker-footed bat (*Myzopoda aurita*) is regarded as rare, but is known from numerous locations throughout the eastern rainforest, although most records are from forest margins and marshlands where traveller's trees are common. The western sucker-footed bat (*M. schliemanni*), smaller and paler, was described in 2006.

Commerson's leaf-nosed bat. Ankarafantsika, Kirindy, Nosy Mangabe and Masoala are good places to look for this species. (DA)

Many smaller bats have large ears and elaborate growths and flaps of skin around their faces (in some species called 'leaf noses'). These are part of the bat's echolocation system, a complex means of navigation which is still poorly understood. The various growths may act as sound splitters, directing the echo of the bat's squeaks – or noises made by its prey – into stereophonic sound to aid direction-finding and the judgement of distances. The 'leaf' and ears function together allowing prey-detection and navigation to take place simultaneously.

Most insectivorous-type bats are rarely encountered as they roost in discreet locations during the day and spend most of the night feeding on the wing. This makes casual observation very difficult. Bat roosts must not be investigated too closely, as all species are very susceptible to disturbance. However, two species in Madagascar are encountered with some regularity. Commerson's leaf-nosed bat (*Hipposideros commersoni*) is often seen hunting along forest pathways at night, periodically landing on tree trunks or branches overhanging the trail. And the Mauritian tomb bat (*Taphozous mauritianus*) often roosts in small numbers on tree trunks or rock faces. Tsingy de Bemaraha and Ankarana are good locations for these and numerous other bat species.

Mauritian tomb bats are often seen on trees in the campsite at Ankarafantsika. (NG)

WHALES AND WHALE-WATCHING

The waters around Madagascar are home to numerous cetaceans (whales and dolphins). Some may be resident year-round, but the majority are migrant visitors. The most frequently seen small species include the common dolphin (*Delphinus delphis*), striped dolphin (*Stenella coeruleoalba*) and bottlenose dolphin (*Tursiops truncatus*). Rarities like the Indo-Pacific humpback dolphin (*Sousa chinensis*) are occasionally sighted. All of these are threatened by hunting or accidental entanglement in commercial fishing gear.

The most important species from a conservation and whale-watching perspective is the humpback whale (*Megaptera novaeangliae*), as the waters surrounding Madagascar are a primary breeding area for this species. In particular the shallow channel between the mainland and Ile Ste Marie, running north into Antongil Bay, is a hotspot from late June to September, when female humpbacks gather to give birth to their calves.

The waters off Ile Ste Marie and in Antongil Bay have become popular places to see these wonderful creatures at close quarters. It is only recently that guidelines to protect and safeguard the wellbeing of the whales have begun to be laid down, with the help of conservation organisations like the Wildlife Conservation Society. There are now reputable operators in these areas who can take tourists to view spectacular displays of whale behaviour from a responsible distance.

Humpback whales frequently show their flukes before diving; the various blotches and marks are as unique as fingerprints and help to identify individuals. (NG)

BIRDS

The helmet vanga is best sought in Masoala and Marojejy, where it is common. (NG)

For its size, and given its unparalleled habitat diversity, Madagascar has a relatively short bird list – just short of 300 at the last count. Yet it is home to at least 37 endemic genera, more than any other country in the African region. Here it is quality rather than quantity that attracts the international birding fraternity. There are estimated to be a total of 107 endemic species (52% of the breeding species) which includes five endemic families. The vast majority are more or less dependent on the native forests or wetlands, with rather few inhabiting the open highlands or urban centres.

Madagascar shares 13 species with the Comoros and seven with the Seychelles. Many of these belong to genera confined to the islands of the western Indian Ocean, such as the vasa parrots, blue pigeons and fodies. Those species present in Madagascar are more plentiful than members of the same genera on the other islands. Among these are the greater and lesser vasa parrots, Madagascar blue pigeon and gaudy Madagascar red fody – often the first birds spotted in Antananarivo during the austral summer.

The little scarlet birds that flash past in the spring and summer are Madagascar red fodies (*top left* JT), *Foudia madagascariensis*, in their bright red breeding plumage. Madagascar bee-eaters (*bottom left* DA) are widespread and seen in open habitats and the endemic Madagascar pygmy kingfisher (*right* PC), *Ispidina madagascariensis*, is also common but more elusive.

Conspicuous and noisy, the crested drongo (*left* NG), *Dicrurus forficatus*, is one of the regional endemics Madagascar shares with the Comoros. The confiding Madagascar magpie-robin (*right* IM), *Copsychus albospecularis*, is known for its sweet song. Males are black with varying amounts of white in their plumage and females are drab browns.

Other widespread, adaptable and easily observed species include the Madagascar kestrel, Madagascar bee-eater, the jewel-like Madagascar malachite kingfisher, Madagascar hoopoe, Madagascar wagtail, Madagascar bulbul, the island's only true sunbirds (souimanga and long-billed green sunbirds), the tiny Madagascar mannikin and Madagascar white-eye.

The ground-rollers (Brachypteraciidae) are an attractive family of colourful, thrush-sized birds that are highly sought-after by visiting birders. There are four rainforest species including the pitta-like ground-roller (*Atelornis pittoides*) and scaly ground-roller (*Brachypteracias squamigera*). They forage on the forest floor, feeding on invertebrates such as snails, centipedes, worms, cockroaches, beetles and also small vertebrates. One species – the highly distinctive long-tailed ground-roller (*Uratelornis chimaera*) – is confined to a narrow range in the southwestern spiny bush (see page 43). Most excavate long nest burrows in streamside banks or the ground, but the more arboreal short-legged ground-roller (*B. leptosomus*) nests beneath tree ferns and in tree cavities up to 30m high.

The secretive scaly ground-roller is best sought in Masoala and Mantadia. (NG)

Considered by many to be the island's most beautiful bird, the pitta-like ground-roller inhabits the rainforest band and also Montagne d'Ambre. (NG/NHPA)

The nine couas, aligned with the Asian malkohas in the subfamily Phaenicophaeinae, are frequently seen, particularly in the breeding season. All couas share two conspicuous characteristics: featherless blue skin around their eyes, and long, broad tails.

The three magpie-sized arboreal species bear a striking resemblance to some of Africa's touracos. Interestingly, the acrobatic blue coua (*Coua caerulea*) and the crested coua (*C. cristata*) both include tree gum in their diet. Terrestrial species behave in a manner reminiscent of American roadrunners, or in some cases Old World pheasants. These include the red-capped coua (*C. ruficeps*) and Coquerel's coua (*C. coquereli*) from western forests, and the running coua (*C. cursor*), all of which have black skin on their rumps which they expose to the early morning sun to warm up. The running coua can sometimes be seen sprinting across roads in the spiny bush, while the largest species – the rather stately giant coua (*C. gigas*) – is often heard before it is seen on the forest floor. The red-fronted coua (*C. reynaudii*) and red-breasted coua (*C. serriana*), also both terrestrial, are found in the eastern rainforests.

The impressive giant coua (*above* NG) is easily seen in Berenty and Zombitse.

Reminiscent of Africa's turacos in appearance and behaviour, the crested coua (*left* NG) has a fantastic vocal repertoire and is easily seen from Berenty to Anjajavy and beyond.

During copulation greater vasa parrots are 'tied' together, much like dogs. Note the hen's bald, yellow-orange head. (JT)

PRIMITIVE PARROTS

To the uninitiated, Madagascar's black vasa parrots (*Coracopsis* spp) hardly merit a second glance, but the breeding behaviour of these drab-looking birds is fascinating. Unlike monogamous parrots elsewhere, greater vasa parrots (*C. vasa*) are highly promiscuous, with the females taking the initiative in courtship. Although smaller, the males have risen to the challenge by evolving a large phallus (an outpocketing of the cloaca) for copulation sessions that can last two hours. Females in breeding condition lose their head feathers and the bald skin turns orange-yellow. They have singing perches adjacent to their tree-cavity nests and it is a case of she who sings loudest attracts the most males (who are then responsible for supplying the food). During the chick-rearing phase females spend up to 60% of their time singing (or screeching).

THE BIRDS AND THE BEAKS

The vangas (Vangidae) are the most celebrated endemic bird family in Madagascar. Had Charles Darwin sailed to Madagascar instead of the Galápagos and seen vangas instead of finches, his thoughts on species and evolution would surely have been similarly provoked. Such is the diversity in size, colour and especially beak shape of the various species that it is hard to imagine they are related at all. Yet characteristic features confirm a common ancestry perhaps similar to the helmet-shrikes and batises of Africa.

Vangas fill niches that are occupied in other parts of the world by woodpeckers, wood-hoopoes, shrikes, tits, treecreepers and nuthatches – all of which are absent from Madagascar. Most vangas are gregarious and are often seen in mixed-species feeding flocks.

The various forms of vanga beaks reflect the size of each species' preferred prey, its location and mode of capture. Larger, shrike-like species, such as the hook-billed vanga (*Vanga curvirostris*), have robust beaks with a characteristic hook at the tip to help them deal with sizeable insects and small invertebrates. The extraordinary helmet vanga (*Euryceros prevostii*; see page 95) is known to feed on small chameleons, frogs, insects, small centipedes and even the occasional scorpion.

Pollen's vanga (*Xenopirostris polleni*) and Lafresnaye's vanga (*X. xenopirostris*) use their laterally flattened beaks to peel bark from dead wood and excavate grubs and invertebrates. Chabert's vanga (*Leptopterus chabert*) is more lightly built and behaves like a flycatcher, snapping up insects on the wing. The largest and most easily identifiable species, the sickle-billed vanga (*Falculea palliata*), is a highly gregarious inhabitant of the western and southern forests. Its noisy babbling, wailing and cackling calls are distinctive. It forages in a similar manner to wood-hoopoes, probing crevices in bark for invertebrates.

Smaller species, including the red-tailed vanga (*Calicalicus madagascariensis*) and recently described red-shouldered vanga (*C. rufocarpalis*), have finer beaks suited to hunting insects in foliage, while the remarkable nuthatch vanga (*Hypositta corallirostris*) forages just as true nuthatches do. Recent taxonomic revisions place Ward's flycatcher (*Pseudobias wardi*) with the vangas.

Clockwise from top left: white-headed vanga (NG), rufous vanga (NG), Pollen's vanga (NG/NPL), red-shouldered vanga (CC/BA), Lafresnaye's vanga (NG) and sickle-billed vanga (JT)

The endangered Sakalava rail frequents wetlands in the west such as Lac Kinkony. (NG)

BACK FROM THE BRINK

Until recently, several of Madagascar's endemic birds were considered to be on the brink of extinction. The Alaotra little grebe (*Tachybaptus rufolavatus*) may well already be extinct. But the recent surge of interest and research in Madagascar has revealed many pleasant surprises.

Madagascar's two eagles are among the world's seven rarest birds of prey. Although usually conspicuous where it occurs, the Madagascar fish eagle (*Haliaeetus vociferoides*) numbers only 100 to 120 pairs (until recently only four of these were in protected areas). Yet they are easily seen in some western protected areas, including Ankarafantsika, Bemaraha, and near Anjajavy.

The enigmatic Madagascar serpent eagle (*Eutriorchis astur*), escaped conclusive detection between 1930 and 1993, then in 1995 its unusual calls became known and it has since been located at several northern and eastern rainforest sites, as far south as Zahamena as well as Anjozorobe and near Lac Bemanevika in the Tsaratanana region.

Another elusive rainforest inhabitant, the Madagascar red owl (*Tyto soumagnei*), was not seen between 1973 and its rediscovery near Andapa in the mid-1990s. Again, this species was overlooked due to its secretive nature. It has since been recorded from Montagne d'Ambre to Mantadia and further south.

The marsh-dwelling Sakalava rail (*Amaurornis olivieri*) also evaded detection for 33 years until a 1995 sighting at Lac Bemamba. This small, chestnut-saddled black rail has since been seen by a number of ornithologists at Lac Kinkony. Its status has been changed from critically endangered to endangered by BirdLife International.

The Sakalava rail shares its western wetland range with the endangered Madagascar teal (*Anas bernieri*) and Madagascar fish eagle. Very little is known, though, of the exceedingly elusive slender-billed flufftail (formerly *Sarothrura watersi*, but now reclassified in a genus of its own, *Lemurolimnas*). This tiny rail is known from two widely separated marshes (at Torotorofotsy and near Ranomafana). In 2011, another rail – the tsingy wood rail (*Mentocrex beankaensis*) was described from a western dry forest

A sensational rediscovery is that of the Madagascar pochard (*Aythya innotata*), previously presumed extinct. Fewer than two dozen were discovered in 2006 on a remote lake and an emergency rescue plan was launched. The breeding programme had successfully quadrupled the world's population of this species by 2013.

Despite continuing habitat loss, new discoveries are not uncommon. The cryptic warbler (*Cryptosylvicola randrianasoloi*) of the eastern rainforests was described as recently as 1995. Shortly afterwards came the red-shouldered vanga, which is found in coral ragg scrub of the remote southwest. Research and comparison of different populations of known birds has also led to some reclassification and additions to the scientific register, such as the subdesert brush warbler (*Nesillas lantzii*) from the arid southwest.

The loud, whistling calls of the unusual Madagascar cuckoo-roller (*Leptosomus discolor*) are a characteristic sound of the Malagasy bush. (NG/NPL)

Grey-headed lovebirds (*left* MG), *Agapornis canus*, at their nest cavity. Sometimes flocks of these birds can be seen together. All female Madagascar paradise flycatchers (*centre* NG), *Terpsiphone mutata*, are rufous, but males may be either rufous, or black and white. Velvet asities (*right* HS), *Philepitta castanea*, are lovely birds of the eastern rainforests. They are remarkable in that they exhibit lek breeding behaviour and polygyny. Breeding males are the pole dancers of the avian world, performing displays such as somersaulting around a perch, or hanging upside down while gaping to impress females. They are the best-known birds to physicists specialising in optic wave studies, because of the composition of their colourful facial skin and caruncles.

Male common sunbird-asity (*Neodrepanis coruscans*). The close resemblance of the rainforest-dwelling common and yellow-bellied sunbird-asities to tiny true sunbirds illustrates convergent evolution. The four asities (Philepittidae) are allied to the broadbills. They show striking differences between males and females. In breeding plumage males of all four species sport near-fluorescent blue and green wattles, caruncles and areas of naked facial skin. (NG)

Subdesert mesite (*left* NG/NPL), *Monias benschi*. The mesites (Mesitornithidae) are a peculiar endemic family (so strange that they may yet prove to belong to an endemic suborder) of ground-dwelling birds, which rarely fly even when pursued by predators. They prefer to freeze, relying on cryptic colouration to help them blend into the background. Three species inhabit the island's main ecotypes: the subdesert mesite is confined to the southwestern spiny bush; the brown mesite (*Mesitornis unicolor*) is a scarce denizen of the eastern rainforests; and the white-breasted mesite (*Mesitornis variegata*) inhabits mostly western seasonally dry forests but is also found in a few rainforests. Uniquely, the subdesert mesite – which unlike its two relatives is strongly dichromatic and has cooperative breeding habits – is able to nest in the middle of the dry season in its harsh, sub-arid habitat.

The impressive and generally wary Madagascar crested ibis (*Lophotibis cristata*) is usually encountered foraging in pairs near forest paths. (NG)

With its long, almost double-jointed legs, the Madagascar harrier hawk (*left* NG/NPL), *Polyboroides radiatus*, can extract prey, such as dwarf lemurs, from holes in trees or rock crevices.
The critically endangered Madagascar fish eagle (*right* NG) is easily seen at Ampijoroa and Anjajavy, where a few pairs are protected.

RHAPSODY IN BLUE

The Madagascar blue pigeon (*top left* DA), *Alectroenas madagascariensis*, is best sought at fruiting trees in and around rainforests. Blue vangas (*top right* PO), *Cyanolanius madagascarinus*, are often seen inspecting hanging clumps of leaves for prey, while blue couas (*bottom* NG),are also typically arboreal.

Stump-tailed chameleon (*Brookesia superciliaris*) (NG)

Madagascar is a paradise for herpetologists (scientists who study reptiles and amphibians) with more than 400 reptile species, and new ones frequently being described. Some 92% are endemic.

While some African species or groups are found in Madagascar, many are notable for their absence. There are no agamas, no wall lizards and no monitors. On land there are no front-fanged venomous snakes, so there are no vipers, cobras or mambas. Pythons are absent too. In fact the closest relatives of some Malagasy species – notably iguanids and boas – are from South America.

Reptiles are good at colonising islands because their impermeable skins are unaffected by seawater and they can survive for long periods without food. Madagascar's colonisers fall into three categories. There are the relatively recent arrivals that are very similar to their cousins on mainland Africa or elsewhere, for instance the Nile crocodile, helmeted freshwater turtle and house geckos. Then there are the ones descended from stock that colonised Madagascar long ago, subsequently radiating into a variety of species. This group includes the chameleons, day geckos and tortoises. And most ancient are the groups with close relatives in South America. The ancestors of these species may have reached Madagascar by a land bridge via Antarctica.

CHAMELEONS

Madagascar is the main centre of diversity for chameleons (family Chamaeleonidae) with about half the world's species, including the world's smallest and largest. Some 82 Malagasy species are known – all endemic – and new ones are still being discovered.

Chameleons are distinctive and specialised lizards, perfectly designed for their arboreal lifestyle. Evolution has adapted their bodies for life in the trees (except in the stump-tailed chameleons; see page 116). Their toes are fused together in two opposing groups like a pair of pliers, perfect for gripping branches. Prehensile tails provide added security and can be coiled up when not in use. The body is narrowed to facilitate movement through tangled branches and this also allows it to absorb heat efficiently by turning broadside to the sun. This shape creates an imposing profile to deter predators and rival chameleons (outside the breeding season they are solitary). When alarmed, a chameleon

A male Parson's chameleon the instant prior to firing its tongue. (NG)

A female Oustalet's chameleon eating a house gecko. While insects dominate their diet, chameleons also prey on other reptiles and even small mammals. (MW)

can puff itself up to look even bigger – an ability which doubles as an effective flotation device (they are good swimmers) or shock absorber (when threatened they will hurl themselves to the ground).

A chameleon's eyes are its most peculiar feature. Large, and protected by circular eyelids that cover all but the pupils, they can be swivelled independently so it can look in two directions at once. This allows the chameleon to stay absolutely still and camouflaged while watching out for potential predators and prey on all sides.

When an insect or other prey is spotted, the chameleon focuses with both eyes so that it can judge distance and bring into action its most specialised feature – its tongue. This rests like a primed harpoon in the bottom of its mouth. When fired at prey, it can extend the length of the chameleon's body in a flash, the muscular tip clamping on like a sticky suction cup and sealing the victim's fate.

Male panther chameleon catching an insect. The tongue shoots out with blinding acceleration. Muscle and energy-storing elastic collagen combine to create an incredibly high-speed catapult mechanism. (NG)

A newly hatched Oustalet's chameleon (DA)

All Malagasy chameleons are egg-laying (oviparous) in contrast to some of their African cousins. Large species such as Oustalet's chameleon (*Furcifer oustaleti*) can produce 60 eggs in a clutch. The female lays these in soft ground then takes no part in the incubation process. Baby chameleons hatch as perfect miniatures of their parents and are soon feeding on tiny insects.

The heavyweight contenders: Oustalet's chameleon (*left* BL) and Parson's chameleon (*right* NG)

Nose-horned chameleon (AVZ)

Brookesia peyrierasi is among the smallest reptiles in the world. (NG)

GOLIATHS AND MIDGETS

Two species vie for the title of world's largest chameleon: Oustalet's chameleon from the drier areas of the west and southwest, and Parson's chameleon (*Calumma parsonii*) from the eastern rainforests, where two subspecies are recognised, both of which are various shades of bright green and turquoise. Male Oustalet's chameleons are dull grey-brown, while females are more colourful – often green with patches of red and yellow. Both these giants can exceed 650mm (26in) from nose to tip of tail.

The nose-horned chameleon (*Calumma nasutum*) is the smallest of the 'typical' chameleons. It rarely exceeds 100mm, and much of that is tail. But most minuscule of all is the recently discovered *Brookesia micra*, which has a total length no greater than 30mm and is currently only known from Nosy Hara on the northwest coast.

111

Male panther chameleon, *Furcifer pardalis*. This blue variety is restricted to the northwest. (BL)

Montane jewel chameleon,
Furcifer campani (NG)

Female Labord's chameleon, extending its throat in threat at the photographer's proximity. (NG)

Furcifer minor, male pursuing female (MB)

A COAT OF MANY COLOURS

A chameleon's ability to change colour is one of its most celebrated attributes. In ancient times they were probably kept as pets in southern Europe: Aristotle described their ability to change colour and Shakespeare and his contemporaries claimed they fed on air (the caged chameleons presumably caught insects that came within tongue-shot). Yet it is a common misconception that colour-change is solely for camouflage. While they can be extraordinarily adept at blending into their background, colour is also a language used to convey emotions, communicate with potential mates and defend territories (the males of some species, on encountering a rival, will instantly erupt into a kaleidoscopic display of anger). It is also a means of regulating body temperature.

These chromatic transformations are achieved by pigment-containing cells beneath the skin, which open and close to expose their colour. The change is controlled by a combination of hormonal and nervous activity. A distressed or angry chameleon opens cells containing the brown pigment (melanin) turning it much darker. When the chameleon relaxes, typically yellow and blue cells combine resulting in calmer shades of green. Sexual excitement produces an explosion of colours and patterns. And at night many chameleons turn very pale, perhaps the result of total relaxation.

A NOSE FOR ALL OCCASIONS

Anything Cyrano or Pinocchio could do, chameleons can do better. Madagascar's chameleons display a fantastic array of weird and wonderful noses, from small rounded bumps to twin prongs and long slender lances. Although often called 'horns', they are in fact scale-covered extensions of the nose known as rostral protuberances. Generally only the males have them, as they are used – like colour – in combat and to impress females.

Noses are useful aids to identification for others of the same species, especially when similar species live in close proximity. Experiments have shown that if its nose is removed, an individual chameleon can be thrown into confusion and is not recognised by others.

Labord's chameleons (*Furcifer labordi*) mating. To avoid confusion and mating with other kinds, chameleon species have each evolved specifically shaped genitals, so the male's penis fits the female of its species like a key in a lock. (BL)

Boettger's chameleon, *Calumma boettgeri* (PB)

Petter's white-lipped chameleon, *Furcifer petteri* (DA)

Rhinoceros chameleon, *Furcifer rhinoceratus* (PB)

Short-horned chameleon, *Calumma brevicorne* (PC)

Horned chameleon, *Furcifer antimena* (NG)

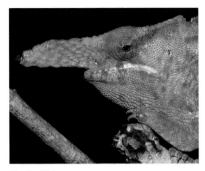

Furcifer bifidus (MB)

Calumma gallus (NG)

Calumma malthe (NG)

Blue-legged chameleon, Calumma crypticum (KL)

Parson's chameleon, Calumma parsonii (DA)

CHAMELEONS IN MINIATURE

The stump-tailed or leaf chameleons (genus *Brookesia*) are the most diminutive, ranging in size from 110mm down to less than 30mm fully grown. The 30 described species are all terrestrial, spending their time in the leaf litter foraging for tiny insects like ants, although some do climb up into the lower twigs of undergrowth to sleep. Their appearance reflects their preferred habitat: they are beautifully camouflaged when among leaves (see page 171). Most inhabit the rainforests, but a few (eg: *Brookesia stumpffi*, *B. decaryi* and *B. perarmata*) are also found in dry deciduous forests.

Brookesia ambreensis (DA)

Brookesia peyrierasi (DA)

Brookesia superciliaris occurs throughout the east. (MB)

Stump-tailed or leaf chameleons possess many of the hallmark chameleon characteristics, including grasping feet, swivelling eyes and a projectile tongue for seizing prey. However, their ability to change colour is limited and their tails are short and not prehensile.

A common trait among the stump-tailed chameleons is their tendency to feign death when threatened. Some fold their legs underneath their bellies and roll onto one side to resemble a dead leaf. Others flatten themselves and produce rapid body vibrations to deter their attacker.

The humid forests of East Africa are home to pygmy leaf chameleons (genus *Rhampholeon*) that exhibit remarkable similarities in appearance and behaviour to *Brookesia* – a good example of convergent evolution.

The giant day gecko is often seen on walks in Ankarana. (DA)

GECKOS

Geckos (infraorder Gekkota) are amongst the most successful of all lizards, with some 1,560 species known worldwide; in Madagascar geckos outnumber all other lizard groups, with 103 species in 11 genera.

The ability of many species to run up vertical surfaces – even glass – is one of their most renowned features. This is achieved by hair-covered pads on each toe that resemble Velcro under the microscope. Some other species are ground-dwellers (eg: the big-headed geckos, *Paroedura* spp) and can be heard at night rustling around in the leaf litter.

Geckos are typically nocturnal, a trait suggested by their large eyes and usually vertical pupils. They do not have eyelids; the eyes are each protected by a single transparent scale which the gecko periodically licks clean with its tongue.

Gecko feet: being ground-dwellers, members of the genus *Paroedura* (*left*) have reduced toe pads and claws; while this *Blaesodactylus* (*right*) gecko is adapted to climb vertical surfaces. (*both* DA)

117

Standing's day gecko (*Phelsuma standingi*) is a rare species restricted to dry forests in the southwest. It is best seen in Zombitse. (NG)

Being active at night there is little need for colour, so most species are dull browns and greys. But there is a glorious exception: one group has reverted to being diurnal. The day geckos (genus *Phelsuma*) have been described as the 'living jewels of Madagascar' and have radiated into some 35 flamboyant and beautiful species. The majority are emerald green with a variety of red, orange, blue or black spots and blotches on their head, back and flanks. The largest is the giant day gecko (*Phelsuma grandis*) which reaches 30cm.

A few nocturnal species are also vocal. Anyone who has spent time in the tropics will be familiar with the chirrups of house geckos (genus *Hemidactylus*). Some forest species like the leaf-tailed geckos (genus *Uroplatus*) and velvet geckos (genus *Blaesodactylus*) can be similarly loud: the distress calls of leaf-tailed geckos when captured by predators are quite blood-curdling.

The fish-scaled geckos (genus *Geckolepis*) are easily identified by their very large overlapping scales. Their response to predators is startling. If seized, they can shed their entire coat of scales in an instant (called autotomy), leaving themselves 'naked', but able to make good their escape. The flayed gecko is a horrendous sight but the scales regenerate within weeks. *Geckolepis maculata* (*left* PS *right* BL)

Unlike most lizards, geckos lay modest clutches of typically one to three eggs. These are round and pea-sized with hard shells (most lizard eggs are soft). They are either hidden in the ground or glued to onto rock faces, beneath tree bark or on the underside of leaves.

Most geckos lay their eggs in twos, often as a fused pair, depositing them in a shady spot on the ground or other surface rather than burying them. Unlike the elongated, leathery-skinned eggs produced by most reptiles, gecko eggs are round and have a hard shell. (DA)

The big-headed geckos (genus *Paroedura*) are a beautifully patterned and diverse group with about 15 species known from rainforest, deciduous forest, spiny bush, and especially around *tsingy* formations. *P. stumpffi* (*above* DA) and *P. picta* (*right* NG)

THE AMAZING UROPLATUS

The leaf-tailed geckos (genus *Uroplatus*) are amongst Madagascar's most extraordinary animals, demonstrating an unparalleled mastery of camouflage. The skin colour and pattern of one of the largest species, *Uroplatus fimbriatus*, for example, mimics its favoured tree trunk. During the day the gecko rests motionless, head downward, stretching out its legs and spatula-like tail and flattening itself against the bark. A frill of skin forms a continuous skirt which blends its outline imperceptibly into the tree. They even possess a limited ability to change colour should they find themselves on lighter or darker bark.

If the camouflage fails, it has another defensive trick up its sleeve. When alarmed it flicks its tail upwards, throws back its head and opens its mouth wide, revealing a brilliant orange-red interior – and sometimes emits a startlingly loud distress call too.

Birds such as couas and large vangas are significant predators, and it is thought that by resting with their heads facing downwards the geckos avoid showing reflections from their eyes. On Nosy Mangabe *U. fimbriatus* is abundant and much more easily found than elsewhere, presumably because of the relative lack of these predatory birds.

At present 14 species are recognised, divided into two groups. The larger species, like *U. fimbriatus*, and the more recently described *U. giganteus*, can measure over 300mm and mimic tree bark. The smaller species, such as *U. phantasticus* and *U. ebenaui*, which are 65mm to 80mm, resemble dry leaves. Leaf-tailed geckos are more diverse and abundant in rainforests, but are also found in deciduous forests.

Leaf-tailed geckos: larger species tend to mimic bark and rest on tree trunks. They also have alarming threat displays.
Top: Uroplatus sikorae (HB)
Left: Uroplatus fimbriatus in defence posture (NG)

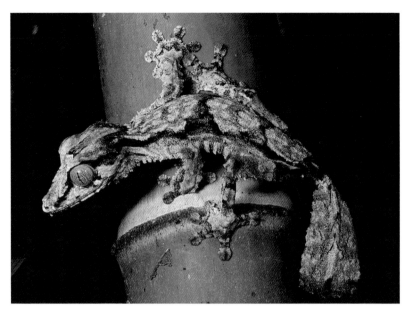

Uroplatus henkeli (NG)

The smaller species (*below*) mimic dead and shrivelled leaves.

Uroplatus alluaudi (DA)

Uroplatus lineatus (NG)   *Uroplatus phantasticus* (NG)   *Uroplatus ebenaui* (NG)

The three-eyed lizard is numerous in most spiny bush areas like Ifaty. (DA)

OTHER LIZARDS

Besides the chameleons and geckos, Madagascar is home to three other families of lizards: the iguanids, plated lizards and skinks.

IGUANIDS

The presence of iguanids (family Iguanidae) is unexpected, as the stronghold of this group is Central and South America. But there is strong evidence to suggest a land bridge briefly existed connecting Madagascar with South America via Antarctica, sometime between 145mya and 65mya, allowing the ancestors of the iguanids to colonise the island.

Oplurus cyclurus (DA)

Madagascar's seven iguanids mainly inhabit the west and southwest, as well as some drier parts of the central highlands. The small three-eyed lizard (*Chalaradon madagascariensis*) is common in the southern spiny bush. Its third 'eye' – a conspicuous black dot on the top of its head – is known as a pineal eye. Although this eye cannot see, it is sensitive to light and contains a lens and retina. It is thought to measure periods of sunlight to regulate daily rhythm.

Spiny-tailed iguanids (genus *Oplurus*) are common in the dry south and west. The tails of two species in particular, *Oplurus cuvieri* and *O. cyclurus*, look like elongated fir cones. The other four species' tails are long but less spiny. They live on rocky outcrops; at least two (*O. quadrimaculatus* and *O. saxicola*) are regularly seen in rocky areas along Route Nationale 7 from Ambositra to Ihosy.

Collared iguanid, *Oplurus cuvieri* (DA)

Zonosaurus madagascariensis (DA)   *Zonosaurus maramaintso* (BL)

PLATED LIZARDS AND SKINKS

The smooth, streamlined lizards belonging to these two families (Gerrhosauridae and Scincidae) are similar in appearance and are often seen darting through the leaf litter. Being slender, they are occasionally mistaken for snakes.

Plated lizards are found throughout eastern and western regions. The most conspicuous belong to the genus *Zonosaurus* of which there are 17 species. Many are beautifully patterned with bold stripes of cream, gold and black. While most live on the ground, there are two bright green arboreal species, *Zonosaurus boettgeri* and *Z. maramaintso*. The latter was described in 2006 and is known only from Bemaraha.

The skinks are a large family of lizards (more than 1,570 species worldwide) normally associated with a terrestrial lifestyle, and many have adapted to burrowing. In Madagascar, 76 species are currently recognised. Many have limbs which are extremely reduced or even completely absent. The cream-and-black striped burrowing skink *Androngo trivittatus* is sometimes seen at Berenty in the leaf litter beneath tamarind trees.

Evolution has reduced the legs of the near-limbless skink *Amphiglossus crenni* to mere rudimentary growths, each with just a pair of toes since they are not useful for its burrowing lifestyle. (HB)

Large ground boas are capable of taking prey as large as lemurs (*Eulemur* or *Hapalemur* spp); smaller individuals feed on rodents and sometimes other reptiles like this iguanid. (NG)

SNAKES

Given its proximity to Africa, it seems remarkable that Madagascar has not been colonised by any of the dangerously venomous snakes that inhabit the mainland. This is an obvious attraction for visitors as forest walks are safe. Only four families are represented on the island: the boas, lamprophids and some rarely seen burrowing snakes (Typhlopidae and Xenotyphlopidae).

BOAS

Boas (family Boidae) are primarily a South American family, although they are represented in Africa by a splinter group of half a dozen species (the sand boas) and by three species in Madagascar.

The largest is the Madagascar ground boa (*Acrantophis madagascariensis*), which resembles the boa constrictor from Central and South America. The Malagasy species is smaller than its cousin, averaging 2–2.5m and occasionally exceeding 3m. Its geometric pattern of browns, creams, greys and black, is excellent camouflage on the leaf litter. Ground boas hunt mainly at night by stealth and ambush and are particularly fond of small mammals, including lemurs.

125

Whilst sometimes seen basking on the ground, the Madagascar tree boa is – as its name suggests – partially arboreal. (BL)

Dumeril's boa (*A. dumerili*) is a closely related species from the drier regions of the south and southwest. It may spend dormant periods in the underground burrows of ant colonies, giving rise to local myths that they enter these nests when young and are fed by the ants until too fat to escape – whereupon the ants eat them!

The Madagascar tree boa (*Sanzinia madagascariensis*) is the smallest and most common boa. There is considerable variation in colour between snakes from different areas: those from the east sport a mosaic of olive green, grey and black, whereas those from western areas tend to be brownish. The two varieties are now considered to be distinct subspecies. The colouration of juveniles is markedly different, being reddish-brown or even orange.

LAMPROPHID SNAKES

The vast majority of snakes in Madagascar belong to this family (Lamprophiidae), until 2010 traditionally treated as part of the colubrid family. Some 81 species in 20 genera inhabit the island, with new ones still being found. Frequently seen are the hognose snakes of the genus *Leioheterodon*. The largest and most common, *Leioheterodon madagascariensis*, is widespread, occurring both in rainforests and dry forests. It is a handsome yellow and black snake up to 150cm. Slightly smaller, *L. geayi* and *L. modestus* are reddish-brown or sand-coloured and are restricted to drier western regions. The 'hognose' peculiar to this genus is a modified scale that allows them to use their snout as a shovel to dig up buried iguanid eggs – a favourite food.

Madagascar hognose snake (DA)

Speckled hognose snake *Leioheterodon geayi* digging for eggs of the collared iguanid. All *Leioheterodon* species are avid egg predators. (*main image* DA) A collared iguanid laying eggs (*inset* BL)

Though harmless, the arboreal *fandrefiala* (*Ithycyphus perineti*) is much feared by some rural Malagasy. They believe it can mesmerise people or cattle passing below, then stiffen and drop tail first, like a spear, impaling its unfortunate victim. The blood-red tail no doubt inspired this myth.

The spear-nosed snake (*Langaha madagascariensis*) looks outlandish even on an island renowned for its bizarre creatures. Both males and females have quite extraordinary noses. The two-tone male's is like a bayonet, while the female – which is disguised effectively as a twig – has a nose like a feathery club. The two other species in this genus (*L. alluaudi* and *L. pseudoalluaudi*) have equally extravagant noses (see page 173).

Perhaps the most frequently seen snake in drier habitats is the slender and speedy *Mimophis mahfalensis*, which is brown and grey with symmetrical patterning. It preys on frogs and small lizards, including chameleons. Also commonly encountered across the island is *Dromicodryas bernieri* – another fast-moving lizard predator.

The exact function of the remarkable 'nose' of *Langaha madagascariensis* is unclear. (BL)

Phisalixella arctifasciatus (*left* DA) and *Lycodryas citrinus* (*right* BL). Members of these nocturnal genera are characterised by very slender bodies, broad heads and huge eyes. They are sometimes called Malagasy cat snakes. Many are exquisitely beautiful.

Many of Madagascar's smaller lamprophid snakes are specialist lizard-eaters. Here *Dromicodryas bernieri* predates upon a *Paroedura bastardi* gecko (*above* DA) and a three-eyed lizard (*right* JT).

Ploughshare tortoises (DA)

TORTOISES AND TURTLES

Madagascar has the dubious distinction of being home to some of the world's rarest tortoises (family Testudinidae). In total there are five species, of which four are endemic. There are also four species of freshwater turtle (families Pelomedusidae and Podocnemididae) and five of marine turtle (families Cheloniidae and Dermochelyidae) in Malagasy waters.

The ploughshare tortoise, or *angonoka* (*Astrochelys yniphora*), is the largest terrestrial species. It is also the rarest, with fewer than 400 remaining in its habitat – a tiny area of deciduous forest near Mahajanga. In recent years the numbers have been augmented by reintroductions from the successful captive-breeding programme at Ankarafantsika run by Durrell Wildlife Conservation Trust.

This species gets its name from the long, upturned spur that projects forward from the plastron (lower shell). Males use this to joust, trying to lever their opponents onto their backs and gain the attention of female onlookers. In an unusually robust form of foreplay, they may also use it to roll the female over several times before mating.

The radiated tortoise (*Astrochelys radiata*) is more common and is found in the south. The name comes from the attractive radiating patterns on its shell. This makes them appealing as pets – sadly a common practice, despite being illegal. The remaining two endemic tortoises are much smaller. The endangered flat-tailed tortoise or *kapidolo* (*Pyxis planicauda*) inhabits dry deciduous forests around Morondava. The extreme climatic conditions of this area force them to aestivate, burying themselves under leaf litter and sand during the dry season; only after substantial rain do they become active. The spider tortoise (*Pyxis arachnoides*) has a wider range, preferring the very dry conditions of the spiny bush. Both species lay a single large egg, up to three times per season. The hinge-back tortoise (*Kinixys belliana*) is the only non-endemic species, occurring on Nosy Faly and the adjacent mainland in northwest Madagascar, as well as throughout much of Africa.

Of the four freshwater turtles, only the Madagascar big-headed (or side-necked) turtle (*Erymnochelys madagascariensis*) is endemic. Its nearest relatives are in South America. This large turtle, with a carapace length up to 410mm, is found in western lakes and waterways, but is now endangered owing to drainage of its wetland habitat for rice production. It is protected by law but unfortunately, since it reaches an edible size long before sexual maturity, many end up in the cooking pot before having the chance to reproduce. However, the breeding project at Ankarafanstsika has released about 100.

Two species of marine turtle are regular visitors to Malagasy waters. The green turtle (*Chelonia mydas*) and hawksbill turtle (*Eretmochelys imbricata*) are both classified as endangered, the latter critically so. They breed on remote beaches of the west coast, where local people still dig up the eggs as a source of food. The most accessible hawksbill turtle nesting site is on Nosy Iranja. When hauling themselves across the sand and depositing eggs, turtles are extremely susceptible to disturbance and should not be approached.

Madagascar big-headed turtle (BL)　　　Radiated tortoise (DA)

FROGS

Frogs (order Anura) are the only amphibians to have colonised Madagascar. There are no newts or salamanders, since they are restricted to the northern hemisphere; nor are there any caecilians. The absence of this group of worm-like amphibians is puzzling, because they are found not only in Africa but also on the nearby Seychelles.

Because of their permeable skins amphibians cannot survive exposure to saltwater, so rafting across oceans presents a huge obstacle. But Madagascar was isolated long before the island's frogs evolved, so some original colonists must somehow have made it across. Consequently, it is no surprise, that very few frog families are represented on the island. This small number of founders evolved and diversified into the spectacular array of frogs we see in Madagascar today. Some 300 species are documented, but with a huge backlog waiting to be described, and more sure to be discovered, the island's true total is likely to exceed 450. All but three of these (all probably introduced by man) are endemic.

Water is central to a frog's lifestyle and breeding, so predictably the eastern rainforests are home to the majority of Madagascar's amphibians. A few, such as *Boophis occidentalis*, have adapted to the drier environments of the west and southwest, particularly in areas that provide pockets of more humid habitat like Isalo and Bemaraha. Some frogs in these areas (genera *Aglyptodactylus* and *Scaphiophryne*) are so-called explosive breeders, remaining dormant for a large part of the year when it is dry and then emerging after the first heavy rains to lay their eggs in mass aggregations.

The painted burrowing frog (or Malagasy rainbow frog), *Scaphiophryne gottlebei*, is critically endangered. This bizarre-looking frog is restricted to the Isalo area. (NG/NPL)

Scaphiophryne madagascariensis retreats underground during the dry season, sometimes burrowing as deep as 50cm. (NG/NHPA)

Aglyptodactylus madagascariensis breed *en masse* after heavy rains, an event for which they turn bright yellow; otherwise they are creamy brown and live among the leaf litter. (*both* DA)

There are other specialists that live only in high montane habitats (above 2,000m) and require very specific environmental conditions to survive. It is thought that some of these are becoming increasingly threatened by global warming; as temperatures rise and climate alters, they need to migrate to higher elevations to find the conditions they require. The risk is that they will soon run out of mountain to ascend and become extinct. Other serious threats to Madagascar's frogs include the recent arrival of chytrid fungus (see page 54), habitat destruction and fragmentation, over-collection for the pet trade (especially *Mantella*, *Scaphiophryne* and *Dyscophus* species) and hunting of larger species for food.

The aptly named tomato frog (*Dyscophus antongilii*) is known mainly from the Maroantsetra area near Masoala. Its bright colour is a warning to predators: if attacked the frog exudes a sticky white secretion which is toxic and can cause swelling. (NG)

Most being nocturnal, frogs rely heavily on sound for communication. Their various chirrups, clicks, squeaks and honks are part of the experience in a Malagasy rainforest, especially after rain. The males call to attract females and warn rival males off their territory, often at a remarkable volume. This is achieved by amplifying the sound using vocal sacs on the throat. Some species have one large sac, while others have a pair of smaller sacs that look like giant cheek pouches when inflated.

A male *Boophis pyrrhus* calling from his leaf perch near a stream. The call of this species has a distinctive metallic tone. (DA)

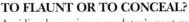

The mottled dark colouration and granular skin of *Gephyromantis boulengeri* helps to blend in with the leaf litter or, in the case of this male, his calling perch. This common species calls during the daytime so relies on its camouflage for protection. (DA)

Pandanus frogs, like this *Guibemantis liber*, live amongst the leaves of screw pines (genus *Pandanus*), retreating into the safety of the plant's rain-filled axils when threatened. (DA)

TO FLAUNT OR TO CONCEAL?

Avoiding becoming a predator's next meal is a major concern for frogs as they are preyed upon by snakes, lizards, birds and mammals. Blending in with their surroundings is a common strategy; nocturnal frogs generally resemble their daytime resting places. Green tree frogs often sleep in a flattened posture on the undersides of leaves. Others (eg: many *Spinomantis* spp) are the frog equivalents of leaf-tailed geckos; their mottled colouration with various spines and fringes helps disguise them as lichen or moss. Most members of the genus *Mantidactylus* are terrestrial, so blend in well with the leaf litter where they spend their day at rest (see page 173).

The opposite strategy is adopted by one of Madagascar's most celebrated groups, the 'Malagasy poison frogs' (genus *Mantella*), which resemble the poison dart frogs (family Dendrobatidae) of Central and South America. Both groups use bright colours to warn potential predators of their toxic skin secretions that render them unpalatable, although none of the 16 mantella species is as poisonous as some of their New World counterparts. Mantellas are primarily terrestrial and, confident in the protection their noxious coats afford, are active by day. At least six mantellas are critically endangered, including the golden mantella (*M. aurantiaca*; see page 21) and harlequin mantella (*M. cowani*).

Mantella baroni (*left* DA) can be seen at Mantadia and at Ranomafana where the very similar painted mantella (*M. madagascariensis*) is also found. Their calls are high-pitched staccato clicks, like two pieces of metal being struck together. The harlequin or Halloween mantella (*right* FA) is one of the rarest amphibians in the world.

The green-backed mantella (*Mantella laevigata*) lays its eggs in rain-filled tree holes and the hollow stumps of giant bamboo. Usually only a single tadpole occupies this microhabitat at any one time, with the mother sometimes depositing unfertilised eggs for her offspring to eat. Neotropical poison dart frogs, although unrelated, exhibit remarkably similar behaviour. (DA)

Some terrestrial frogs have false 'eyes' (inguinal spots) on their lower backs. When these frogs raise themselves up in a defensive posture, these create the impression of a much larger animal.

TREE FROGS

Most tree frogs have large discs on tips of their fingers toes to help them grip leaves, and big eyes for night vision. But to find them you must be prepared to spend many hours in the rainforest at night, systematically homing in on their calls. Rainy nights are the most rewarding.

Typical of tree frogs is the genus *Boophis*, containing some 75 species, many of which breed in fast-moving streams. They range in colour from dull creams and browns to vibrant greens and reds. Many have colourful eyes, which may be another anti-predator tactic; when resting during the day the vivid colour is hidden, but when disturbed the frog instantly opens its eyes wide, flashing the warning.

Boophis luteus (*top left*) is a large arboreal species, often encountered at Andasibe and Ranomafana. The white-lipped tree frog, *Boophis albilabris* (*left*) is a giant amongst tree frogs, sometimes exceeding 8cm. It has very well-developed webbing on the hands and feet and is usually found high up in vegetation near streams. *Boophis madagascariensis* (*top right*) is perhaps the most frequently seen of Madagascar's large tree frogs. In common with most arboreal species it has enlarged fingertips to assist in climbing. (*all* DA)

A characteristic feature of *Boophis viridis* is its intensely blue eyes. (DA)

Boophis bottae (*left* NG) was described in 2002. Both this colourful species and the very similar *B. rappiodes* are found at Andasibe and Ranomafana. A *Boophis brachychir* froglet (*right* DA) in the final stages of metamorphosis. Its tadpole tail has all but disappeared and the iridescent gold colour will also fade as it enters the adult phase.

The Betsileo reed frog (*Heterixalus betsileo*) inhabits the marshes and rice paddies of the central highlands. (DA)

Another colourful group are the reed frogs (genus *Heterixalus*). Most of the 11 known species are green or yellow with orange feet and conspicuous stripes and squiggles on their backs and flanks. A notable exception is *Heterixalus alboguttatus*, one of the larger species, sometimes seen at Ranomafana. The females are blue-black with pale yellow spots. Viewed in sunlight, however, the blue is deeper and the yellow spots are more vibrant with black rings.

Colouration of the Madagascar reed frog (*Heterixalus madagascariensis*) is very changeable, appearing various shades of blue, yellow or white. In areas of high rainfall along the east coast it is a fairly common species, which can tolerate degraded habitats. (DA)

INVERTEBRATES

This spectacular stick insect is well camouflaged, and the stout leg spines usually deter predators. If this fails, it flashes a bright warning using specially modified wings. Stick insects are disguised during the day and feed, mostly on leaves, at night. (MG)

Invertebrates (animals without backbones) comprise more than 95% of all animal species on earth. Those found in Madagascar are astonishingly diverse and beautiful. There are thought to be at least 100,000 species, including beetles, butterflies, spiders, scorpions, crabs, flatworms, leeches, millipedes (160 species), snails (685), ants (1,000), flies (1,800) and a myriad of other groups. Invertebrate hunters in Madagascar certainly do not run the risk of boredom!

All Madagascar's invertebrates play an important role in the island's ecology, and there are fascinating explanations for their often peculiar forms and behaviour.

IN AND OUT OF HIDING

In this chapter we divide invertebrates into two groups based on their appearance – those that hide and those that don't. We will take a closer look at how their extraordinary adaptations and designs help them to survive.

The black-and-white wing pattern breaks up this bug's outline, making it harder for predators to spot this potential meal. (MG)

IN HIDING

Every animal wants to eat and avoid being eaten. This simple fact explains why thousands of Madagascar's invertebrates exhibit such remarkable camouflage. Most are hiding from predators by mimicking something of little interest to their enemies, such as a leaf. Others, like praying mantises, hide in order to ambush prey, hoping they won't be seen until it's too late for their victim.

Clear wings make insects harder to see – a good safety measure (*left* IM). Recently discovered and endemic to Madagascar, dracula ants (genus *Adetomyrma*) live up to their name. Queens and workers chew holes in their own larvae and dine on their blood. Despite this, the larvae thrive quite admirably. (*right* BF)

Flatid leaf bugs. These remarkable bugs are quite easy to find in the wet season. The adults look like pink flowers (and a green form looks just like leaves). The nymphs excrete a white waxy substance which 'grows' from the animal like long wispy feathers. If a bird or other predator makes a grab for one of these insects it gets a beakful of white nothing, and the animal jumps to safety with a flea-like hop. They can be seen at Berenty, but a much bigger and more impressive form is found in the western forests. The nymphs also excrete a sugary substance which solidifies in lumps on leaves – a candy treat which is eaten by mouse lemurs. (*left* NG *others* MG.)

Giant bush-cricket. These leaf-mimicking insects are very hard to find, unless they come to a light at night. (LdB)

Adult cicada (DA)

This giant bush-cricket (*left* NG) and cicada (*right* DA) are shedding their skins. Invertebrates with exoskeletons can only grow to a certain size before their inflexible skin prevents further growth. Having shed their old skin they are very vulnerable until new skin hardens, so shedding is often done at night in sheltered places.

Hissing cockroaches, *Gromphadorhina portentosa* (male on hand, female on tree with ovipositor extended). Hissing cockroaches really do hiss (by forcing air through pores in their abdomen) to scare off enemies and settle territorial disputes. Males also fight, ramming one another with the horns above their heads. Although amazingly large (around 7cm), they are relatively slow-moving and cannot fly. They keep themselves very clean and, like the majority of the world's cockroaches, stay out of houses (of some 4,500 species worldwide, fewer than 30 are considered pests). (*left* MG *below* LdB)

OUT OF HIDING

By boldly displaying bright and contrasting colours, many invertebrates warn birds and other predators that they contain toxins that render them inedible. Some non-toxic mimics look distasteful, and because they resemble poisonous species most predators avoid them. Yet other mimics are disguised as food, and will trap and eat animals that come close to investigate.

Scare tactics offer another successful strategy; some invertebrates want to be seen because they look like something you wouldn't want to mess with. The emperor moth (see page 148) is a prime example; eye spots on its wings give the impression of a larger, fiercer animal. Invertebrates also use bright colours to attract and respond to potential mates. This is especially important in dark forests to help males and females find one another.

Jewel beetle (*above* LdB). Naturalist J B S Haldane noted 'God has an inordinate fondness for beetles'. From iridescent jewel beetles like this one to flashy fruit chafers, there may be over 20,000 beetle species in Madagascar, most of which are endemic. An inordinate fondness indeed.
Twig wilters (*below* DA) specialise in sucking sap from twigs and are often found on forest margins.

Giraffe-necked weevil (*Trachelophorus giraffa*). These extraordinary weevils are invariably found on the leaves of *Dichaetanthera cordifolia* on which it feeds. The male's long neck is adapted for rolling a leaf to make an egg case in which the female (which has a shorter neck) lays a single egg. They are easily seen at Ranomafana where they are so popular with tourists that local craftspeople carve wooden ones to sell as souvenirs. (NG)

Shield bug (*left* NG). The bright colours warn that the bug will emit a foul smell if attacked or handled. Many of Madagascar's 200 or so species are quite large and gorgeously coloured, so are easy to find. The vivid orange and black colouration of this predatory assassin bug (*right* MG) warns that it delivers a vicious bite.

Caterpillars' colourful spines are usually a defence mechanism. They often contain a powerful irritant, and the bright body colour is a further warning. (*bottom left* IM *others* DA)

Bold stripes may reveal *or* hide – some stripes break up a caterpillar's outline, making it harder for birds to see. (*bottom right* LdB *others* DA)

Comet moth (*Argema mittrei*). These handsome moths, whose caterpillars spin equally beautiful silvery cocoons, are much bigger (by a third) than their African relatives. They are bred commercially in Madagascar for collectors. (NG)

Emperor moths mimic a large predator, such as an owl, in the hope of scaring off potential threats. The bold red flash colouration is an additional warning. Once danger has passed, the moth will cover its hind wings and pretend to be a dead leaf. (NG)

Urania or sunset moth (*Chrysiridia rhipheus*). At first glance this diurnal moth looks like a butterfly. It feeds on the four endemic species of *Omphalea*, which are so toxic that few other animals can eat them. This moth is closely related to the genus Urania of South America, which also eat *Omphalea*; one species of *Chrysiridia* also occurs in Tanzania. (PB)

Cyligramma disturbans. This beautiful moth inhabits dark places such as caves and the rainforest understorey. Many Malagasy believe them to be the embodiment of their ancestors, so it is *fady* (taboo) to kill them. More than 4,200 Malagasy moth species are known. (DA)

The false eye spots at the base of the hindwings of this butterfly (family Nymphalidae) draw a predator's attention away from its head. A butterfly can still fly with a damaged hindwing, but a peck to the head will kill it. (LdB)

Atrophaneura anterior, Madagascar's largest butterfly. The presence of this swallowtail is puzzling since its closest relatives occur in southeast Asia. (*left* HB *right* NG)

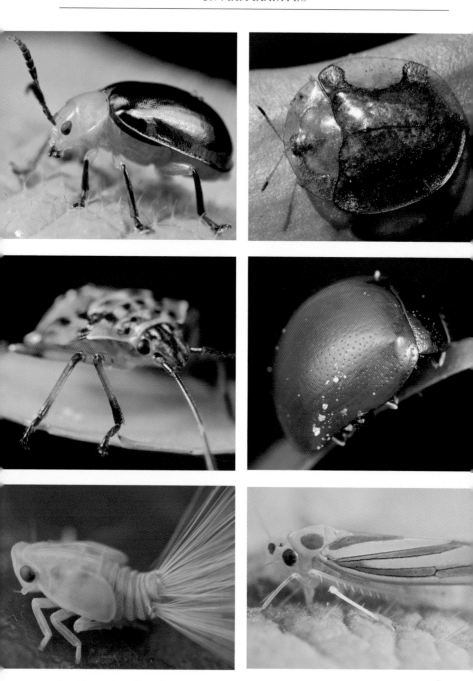

Invertebrates abound in endless variety. *Clockwise from top left:* shiny leaf beetle, golden tortoise beetle, red and black seed beetle, cicadellid leafhopper, leafhopper nymph and blue shield bug. (*top right* LJ, *others* PB)

Clockwise from top left: male lobster jumping spider, multicoloured cricket, mating rainbow milkweed locusts, katydid nymph, and cotton stainer bug. (*bottom right* DA, *others* PB)

Comet orchid (NG)

THE ORCHID AND THE MOTH

The delicately perfumed, white *Angraecum* orchids of Madagascar are one of the botanical delights of the island. The most famous is the comet orchid, *Angraecum sesquipedale*.

Some of the British missionaries who worked in Madagascar in the 19th century found the study and recording of the island's natural history a fascinating diversion, especially while travelling through the eastern rainforests *en route* to the capital from the port of Tamatave. The Reverend William Ellis described the comet orchid in his book *Three Visits to Madagascar during the Years 1853-1854-1856*, published in 1859. He later brought it to Britain where James Bateman, a well-known horticulturist, cultivated it and sent Charles Darwin some specimens.

In his 1862 book *On the Various Contrivances by which British and Foreign Orchids are Fertilised by Insects*, Darwin wrote: '*Angraecum sesquipedale's* large six-rayed flowers, like stars formed of snow-white wax, have excited the admiration of travellers in Madagascar. A whip-like green nectary of astonishing length hangs down beneath the labellum. In several flowers sent me by Mr Bateman I found the nectaries eleven and a half inches long, with only the lower inch and a half filled with nectar. What can be the use, it may be asked, of a nectary of such disproportional length? We shall, I think, see that the fertilisation of the plant depends on this length, and on nectar being contained only within the lower and attenuated extremity. It is, however, surprising that any insect should be able to reach the nectar: our English sphinxes have probosces as long as their bodies; but in Madagascar there must be moths with probosces capable of extension to a length of between ten and eleven inches [25–28cm]!' In the 1877 edition, Darwin added: 'This belief of mine has been ridiculed by some

Darwin moth (NG)

entomologists, but we now know from Fritz Müller that there is a sphinxmoth in South Brazil which has a proboscis of nearly sufficient length.'

Some two decades after Darwin's death, a moth with a proboscis of 30cm was finally discovered in Madagascar. It was named *Xanthopan morgani praedicta* in honour of his prediction. Recently, scientists used infrared cameras to capture it on film visiting a comet orchid – irrefutable proof of the relationship between moth and flower.

MILLIPEDES

Giant millipedes (*left and below*) may exceed 15cm. Their many legs enable them to cover all sorts of terrain – including vertical climbs – at a steady pace. The red colour warns potential predators that they are foul-tasting, yet lemurs have been known to eat them, wiping the secretions onto their tails. A female black lemur at Lokobe was seen to nip a millipede and then float off into a trance while rubbing the toxin-loaded exudates over her front and tail. It is thought these millipedes may act as an insecticide as well as a drug. (*both* DA)

Unlike centipedes, which deliver a painful bite, millipedes are harmless to humans and attractive. Pill millipedes (genus *Sphaerotherium*) come in a variety of colours and can roll themselves into an impregnable ball when threatened. (*left* LdB *right* DA)

SPIDERS

Of all invertebrates, spiders exhibit some of the most extravagant and bizarre behaviour and designs. From bird-dropping mimics that look (and probably smell) like a tasty meal for a hungry fly, to massive golden orb-weavers where the female can weigh a thousand times more than the male, spiders are always worth a closer look.

The cannibalistic archaea, or pelican spider, specialises in eating other spiders (see page 24 for photo). Its long neck and massively elongated jaws are a design feature enabling it to strike from a distance. Archaea was long considered an extinct oddity before being discovered alive and well in Madagascar. Some 35 living species are now described – most from Madagascar.

There are over 470 known species of spider on the island, but the true number may exceed 3,000. In 2007 a curious tourist snapped a picture of a spider which experts have yet to place in a family, let alone identify the genus or species!

SEX AND THE SINGLE SPIDER

Like all animals, spiders have two major preoccupations: food and sex. Among spiders, these two drives are in uneasy conflict. A mature female's prime concern is eating, while the male is more interested in mating. Since the male is often much smaller than the female, she may mistake him for a meal, so he has to go to considerable effort to achieve his goal without being eaten. He begins by depositing sperm on a special web before transferring it to a modified leg called a pedipalp. Then comes the tricky part – getting it inside the female. Some tap out a code on the web to announce their presence; others do an elaborate dance, or present the female with a tasty morsel to distract her. And sometimes, like the male golden orb-web spider, he may simply be so tiny that he would barely be a snack worth bothering with.

Golden orb-web spider, *Nephila madagascariensis* (*left* NG). Their massed, semi-communal webs are an unmistakable feature of many Malagasy towns, where these harmless spiders perform the service of catching and devouring millions of flies, mosquitoes and other pests. The silk of these webs is as tough as nylon, and indeed a textile industry using spider silk was attempted towards the end of the 19th century. Green lynx spider, *Peucetia madagascariensis* (*right* JR) is an endemic species found in the eastern forests. These fast-moving spiders do not inhabit a typical web, but are 'wait-and-pounce' hunters.

Common in the eastern forests, these orb-web spiders are seen in a wide variety of colours and shapes, but all appear to belong to the same species. (DA)

Net-throwing spider. This is a widespread family of nocturnal spiders with an extraordinarily elaborate – and effective – method of catching their prey. The spider first weaves a rectangular web of various types of silk, most of which are highly elastic. When this net is finished, the spider grasps each corner in its four front legs, cuts the web free from its supports, and hangs head downward with the net at the ready. If an insect passes by, either on the wing or on foot, the spider lunges at it like a butterfly collector, the net being stretchy enough to enmesh even quite large prey. (BL)

Kite or thorn spiders are well known in Africa, and there are many colourful species and an endemic subspecies in Madagascar. (IM)

The hunting strategy of this bird-dropping spider (genus *Phrynarachne*) is to sit on a leaf mimicking excrement and to grab any fly that takes a close interest. Note the white threads on the leaf which make it look more like the white of bird faeces, and the glistening dropping-like abdomen of the spider. It is thought they also release a scent resembling fresh dung. (JR)

A large mygalomorph spider in a cave at Ankarana (DA)

Body coverings like on this species (*Magel*) are usually protective – any predator foolish enough to try a bite may end up with a mouthful of strongly irritant hairs. (BL)

OTHER LAND INVERTEBRATES

Many crabs in Madagascar are found far from water in the moist forests, where they can get enough moisture from their damp environment. (*above* MG)

Scorpion (*Grosphus palpator*). For visitors, scorpions are effectively the only dangerous animals in Madagascar. They are active after rain and at night. During the day they like to hide under stones or in crevices – beware! Boots or rucksack pockets are favoured places. Watch out for those like this *Grosphus* with a massive tail and thin pincers; this shows they have a potent venom with which to kill prey. The sting of larger species from the western forests is excruciatingly painful to adults and can kill a child. Scorpions with thick pincers and a thin tail are usually less venomous, and rely on the strength of their pincers to kill their prey. All Malagasy scorpions are endemic. (*below* NG/NPL)

A snail from the eastern rainforests (*above left* LdB). This one is well-camouflaged in the leaf litter. Many snails live on trees – try looking for them in the forests at night.

Giant land snails mating (*above right* DA). These huge snails, whose shells litter some forest floors, were introduced from Africa. Indirectly, they nearly caused the extinction of many of the native snails. Madagascar's snails are of great interest to naturalists because there are so many species (probably close to 400) and most are endemic.

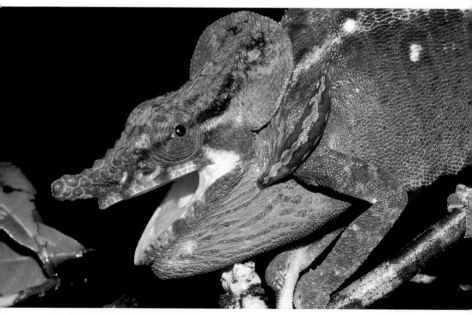

Madagascar's leeches are small and do not live in water but hang around on bushes waiting for a passing host – this could be a chameleon as shown here (*Calumma malthe*) or perhaps a tourist! They attach themselves to their victim with a tail-end sucker and inject an anticoagulant into the wound made with their sharp jaws. The bite is usually painless but the result is messy. Once the leech has had its fill it falls off, but the bitten area can itch for several days. Leeches are mostly gut: pouches all down the digestive tract enable the animal to hold a large quantity of blood. A satiated leech is about four times its hungry size. At least it does not need to feed again for several months; it will take a long time to digest this banquet of blood. (DA)

Above: This impressive animal is not a leech but a flatworm. Madagascar has several species, many of which are brightly coloured with two-tone stripes running down their bodies. All have hammer-shaped heads and are harmless. Like most soft-bodied invertebrates, they are most commonly encountered after rain. Dry conditions force them to retreat into moist hiding places to avoid dehydration.
Left: Madagascar has some impressively large earthworms, some approaching a metre long. These are a favourite food of tenrecs. (*both* DA)

Termites are also devoured by tenrecs as well as forming a large part of the diet of many other mammals, birds, reptiles and amphibians. Some 50 species of termite are known from Madagascar (of which about a third are endemic to the island) but they have been little studied, so there are no doubt many new species awaiting discovery. Termites live in large colonies with a similar social structure to that of ants, although the two groups are not closely related. Termite colonies comprise five types of individual: queens, kings, alates (winged reproductives of both sexes), soldiers and workers. Kings and queens form monogamous pairs, and large colonies of some species may have more than one royal pair. (DA)

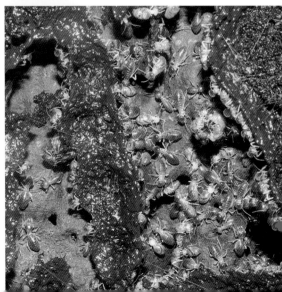

INVERTEBRATE CONSERVATION ISSUES

There are many invertebrates for sale at markets, especially around Antananarivo. The question is: for how long can their populations sustain the pressure? Big beetles like the spectacular longhorns may spend years as larvae boring through wood before becoming adults. While few of these insects seem to be farmed sustainably, many Malagasy families make their living from these sales.

Freshwater crayfish are an important food and income source for local communities. But there is concern that the six endemic species are being overexploited, and a recent study has found that they only occur in streams that are flanked by natural vegetation.

Mounted butterflies (*left*) and other invertebrates are often available as souvenirs. The solitaire game below is sold with 38 different species of beetle set inside the balls. (*both* LdB)

WHERE, WHEN AND HOW TO LOOK FOR INVERTEBRATES

The wonderful thing about invertebrates is that you can find them everywhere. You do not need to visit a national park or reserve, and even a brief stroll around a local roadside will reveal something special. Keep a sharp eye out wherever you find yourself.

Expect huge variation in invertebrates as you move from one habitat to another. Rainforests will yield totally different species from the spiny bush, and you will be surprised how much you find even in the towns and cities.

Where and When

Ponds and rivers are great places to start – you should see many dragonflies and their slower-flying relatives, damselflies.

Look around lights at night, especially in the national parks. Hang a white shirt or sheet next to the light to make it more visible. Particularly rewarding are moths, especially the large and spectacular emperor moths (family Saturniidae) with false eye spots on the wings. Different insects emerge at different times of night, so if you're up at 04.00 check the lights to see what's there.

Lift rocks and logs (slowly, and away from you) to find scorpions, beetles, flatworms, millipedes, spiders and other delights. Carefully replace the log or rock after looking.

Find a tree that is in flower or has ripe fruit. You are likely to see butterflies, beetles and numerous other glorious invertebrates, not to mention the many birds that come to eat them.

Look *underneath* leaves and on tree trunks to make further discoveries. It is almost certain that any rainforest tree will be home to several invertebrates you have not seen... yet.

On sunny days, the tops of small hills are great places to see insects. Many species congregate there to display, meet and mate. Dragonflies, chafer beetles (family Cetoniidae) and Butterflies particularly like 'hilltopping'.

Sunny patches in forests are rich 'super bowls' which have heat, stillness, moisture and food – the perfect environment for invertebrates.

Simple Tools

A magnifying glass and paper plate are useful. Use the plate to put your finds on and study them closer with the magnifying glass. Release them where you found them once you have finished looking. A handy trick is to hold the paper plate under a leafy branch, then shake it and see what lands on the plate. But be cautious about doing this in protected areas; removing animals from reserves is forbidden and you risk arrest if mistaken for a collector.

A head torch is great at night, and much more effective than a hand-held one. The eyes of many invertebrates reflect straight back to the light source on your head, so you will see them glinting like tiny lights.

THE MALAGASY AND THEIR ENVIRONMENT

Slash-and-burn (*tavy*) (NG)

Madagascar annually goes up in flames. Over the centuries the forest that cloaked the vast majority of the island when the first people arrived some 2,000 to 3,000 years ago has been destroyed to make way for crops and cattle. Folklore and tales of the great fires that raged across the island about a thousand years ago persist to this day.

For its size Madagascar is not overpopulated. In 2014, just over 23 million people lived on an island more than twice the size of Great Britain – a population density of 39 people per square kilometre (compared with Britain's 267).

But in the past 30 years Madagascar's population has more than doubled and its remaining forest area has halved. Now less than 10% of the original forest cover remains, and the fertile soil beneath has been eroded and washed away. Much of the once-forested highlands are a barren wasteland where little of use will grow. The deciduous forests of the west, more vulnerable to fire than the rain-soaked east, are disappearing faster than any other habitat. And in 20 years there will be another 12 million mouths to feed.

A green turtle – illegally caught in the southwest – is tied up alive to keep the meat fresh. (DA)

Destruction of habitat is the main threat to Madagascar's wildlife, although hunting for bushmeat is now also known to be a serious issue. Wild (and endangered) animals, like larger lemurs, small carnivores, bats and tenrecs, provide invaluable protein to many extremely poor people living in rural regions. In some areas local beliefs and taboos (*fady*) still prohibit the killing of certain species. But as people migrate around the island more, and traditional beliefs break down, the wildlife is targeted and put further at risk. Madagascar's future is in the hands of the Malagasy. But to a hungry man it is the present that matters, not the future.

MADAGASCAR AT NIGHT

Brown mouse lemur (DA)

Chameleons are easier to see at night because they turn a much lighter shade, some almost white. This juvenile Parson's chameleon (see page 111) is in a typical sleeping posture with tail tightly coiled. (DA)

FROM DUSK TO DAWN

One of the pleasures of walking in a Malagasy forest is the relative safety: there are no large animals hiding behind trees, no venomous snakes concealed in the foliage and almost no horrible creepy-crawlies lurking in the undergrowth (scorpions are the exception). To add to the excitement, the day and night shifts are completely different. Come dusk, when all the familiar daytime creatures are bedding themselves down, a new cast of characters is stirring. These include nocturnal lemurs, carnivores, nocturnal birds, leaf-tailed geckos, frogs and a myriad of insects. They are Madagascar's spirits of the night.

Of course, the fundamental problem in seeing nocturnal animals is the dark. However, there are telltale signs to look out for. The back of the eye in many nocturnal animals is highly reflective. This specialised area behind the retina, the tapetum lucidum, increases the sensitivity of the eye to dim light. It also reflects incoming light straight back out again so, providing you have a head torch (or hold your torch at eye level), the eyes of an animal looking towards you appear to glow red or green in the beam. This is known as eyeshine.

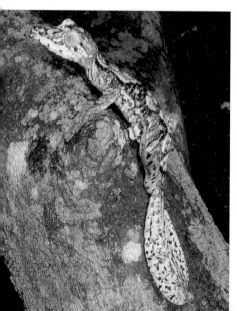

Leaf-tailed geckos (see page 120), like this *Uroplatus giganteus*, are nocturnally active. You are much more likely to spot them at night than during the daytime. (BL)

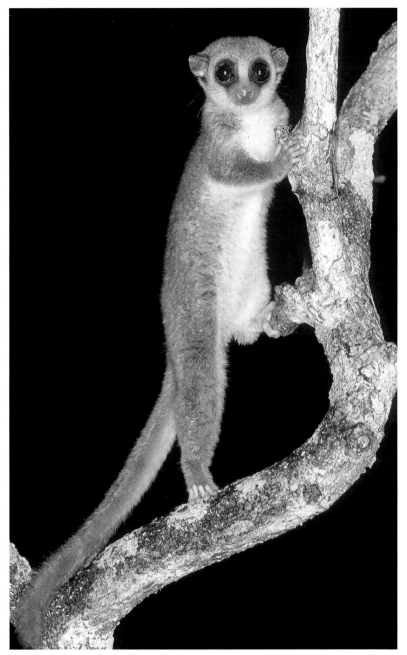

Fat-tailed dwarf lemurs (see page 77) are one of several species of lemur that are nocturnal. Many of Madagascar's most interesting animals may only be seen at night. Guided night walks are usually rewarding at most parks and reserves. (HS)

A SHOT IN THE DARK

Night-time wildlife-watching (and photography) is not just a case of where to look but how to look. Here are some hints.

- Try to avoid times of the full moon. Some animals will be in hiding.
- Wear appropriate clothing: rustle-free fabrics are good.
- Use a head torch in conjunction with a powerful hand torch. Good LED lights throw the most powerful beams. Do not shine these directly into animals' eyes.
- Bring binoculars. They are helpful even in torchlight.
- The first two hours after dark are best. Nocturnal animals have just woken up so are more active and often encountered. Later at night many go back to sleep.

Now you are ready, start by using only the head torch and set the beam focus so that it throws a fairly wide and diffuse pool of light. Then search the lit area using your peripheral vision; that is, avoid looking directly at something of interest. In dim light you will actually see more clearly out of the corner of your eye.

If something catches your attention – a pair of red glowing eyes, for instance – illuminate it fully with the hand torch and check it out using binoculars. Should the animal take flight, shut down the lights, wait and start again – it may resettle close by. Here's where to look for your favourite creatures:

Lemurs

The smaller species (mouse and dwarf lemurs) can be seen anywhere, but it is best to concentrate on the lower, thinner branches that they prefer. Sportive lemurs and woolly lemurs are generally found clinging to narrower vertical trunks. Always investigate the areas around tree holes, especially at dusk when animals have just woken up.

Chameleons

These often sleep at the ends of thin branches, and their pale night-time colour stands out in a torch beam. Check the lower branches around the outside of bushes and trees. Stump-tailed chameleons are found low down or on the ground.

Leaf-tailed Geckos

The larger species, like *Uroplatus fimbriatus* and *U. sikorae*, hunt from ground level to the canopy. Their eyes do shine red, but not as brightly as those of lemurs, and you will only see one eye at a time. The smaller species, like *U. ebenaui* and *U. phantasticus*, tend to be on finer branches of undergrowth and among leaves.

Frogs

Many species are vocal at night, so they are heard but not always seen. They often sound closer than they actually are. Frogs are always more active and vocal after rain and areas near to water are best; investigate the vegetation close to forest streams.

Birds

Go out a couple of hours before dawn. You can then catch the nocturnal birds and be on the spot at daybreak when the diurnal species are at their most active.

Invertebrates See page 163.

CAMOUFLAGE

Collared nightjar (NG)

SAFETY MATCHES

Although the number of true carnivores in Madagascar is relatively few (just 11 species), plenty of other species survive by eating other animals. As predators evolve more effective ways of hunting, prey species endeavour to keep a step ahead. An obvious way to do this is by not being seen in the first place, and numerous species have evolved spectacularly convincing camouflage.

The collared nightjar (*Caprimulgus enarratus*) is nocturnal and spends the day roosting among leaf litter, making it potentially vulnerable to predators. It has intricately patterned plumage that matches the background of dry leaves, moss and twigs, and like so many well-camouflaged animals they are able to keep remarkably still when danger is near, only taking flight when the threat gets uncomfortably close.

Cryptic colouration like that of nightjars or the Madagascar ground boa ensures that the animal blends with its background. Other animals take this a stage further by evolving body parts or adornments that look like elements of their habitat such as leaves, twigs, bark or even flower petals. Madagascar is home to a particularly impressive selection of creatures that have perfected the art of deception. These include, a variety of insects, particularly bush crickets and mantids, tree frogs and forest-floor frogs, small chameleons, and perhaps most spectacular of all, the leaf-tailed geckos (genus *Uroplatus*), as well as some birds and snakes.

Cryptically coloured Madagascar ground boa (*Acrantophis madagascariensis*) (NG)

Short-nosed chameleon blending with the foliage to avoid being seen. (NG)

Some leaf-tailed geckos, like this *Uroplatus ebenaui*, mimic leaves . . . (NG)

. . . while others, such as *Uroplatus sikorae*, look like moss or bark. (DA)

Stump-tailed chameleon (*Brookesia stumpffi*) (DA)

Stick insect (DA)

The rarely seen twig-mimic snakes, *Langaha alluaudi* and *L. pseudoalluaudi* (*above*), have extraordinary noses. This female was spotted during a tourist nature walk in Anjajavy, showing anyone can have the good fortune to see some of Madagascar's rarest animals if they are in the right place at the right time. (HB)

Gephyromantis webbi blending into a mossy rock (DA)

Gephyromantis luteus is difficult to spot in the leaf litter. (DA)

The thorax and abdomen of this mantis are curled and leaf-like. Its leg extensions further break up its outline and it moves like a leaf in the wind. (DA)

FURTHER INFORMATION

Many of the items below are available through your local bookshop or online book retailer. For the specialist titles try **www.nhbs.com**.

Visit **www.madagascar-library.com** for more details and information on the latest publications.

TRAVEL GUIDES

Madagascar (11th ed). Daniel Austin & Hilary Bradt (2014). Bradt Travel Guides. The most comprehensive general travel guide to the country.

Globetrotter Travel Pack: Madagascar (3rd ed). Derek Schuurman & Nivo Ravelojaona (2013). New Holland. A photo-led travel guide aimed at the ecotourist; the only guidebook with a Malagasy co-author.

NATURAL HISTORY
General

The Natural History of Madagascar. Steven Goodman & Jonathan Benstead, eds (2007). University of Chicago. A huge compendium of essays by some 300 experts in all areas of Malagasy natural history. Now available affordably in softback.

Mammals

Mammals of Madagascar: A Complete Guide. Nick Garbutt (2007). A&C Black. A comprehensive guide to the island's mammals. Illustrated with the author's colour photos and detailed ink drawings. Distribution maps and recommended viewing sites for all species.

Lemurs of Madagascar (3rd ed). Russell Mittermeier et al (2010). Conservation International (Tropical Field Guide Series). Excellent reference but too heavy to be used as a true field guide. Many illustrations and photos. Nick Garbutt, co-author of this book, is one of the contributors.

Lemurs of Madagascar: Pocket Identification Guide. Russell Mittermeier et al (2008). Conservation International (Tropical Pocket Guide Series). Laminated checklist with 120 colour drawings for field identification and 94 distribution maps. Also available in separate diurnal and nocturnal editions.

Birds

The Birds of Madagascar: A Photographic Fieldguide. Pete Morris & Frank Hawkins (1998). Pica Press. A comprehensive review of the island's avifauna, covering all species recorded on the island to date. Fully descriptive text illustrated with 500 colour photos.

A Photographic Guide to Birds of the Indian Ocean Islands. Ian Sinclair, Olivier Langrand & Fanja Andriamialisoa (2006). Struik. Bilingual English/French guide to 126 of the most frequently seen Indian Ocean species, with colour photos.

Birds of the Indian Ocean Islands (2nd ed). Ian Sinclair & Olivier Langrand (2003). Struik. A lavishly illustrated guide to 359 birds of the reigon. No photos but numerous drawings with handy quick-reference chart and distribution maps.

Bird Sounds of Madagascar. Frank Hawkins & Richard Ranft (2007). British Library. Audio CD with calls of 127 species.

Bird Sounds of Madagascar, Mayotte, Comoros, Seychelles, Reunion, Mauritius and Rodrigues. P Huget & C Chappuis. SEOF. Bilingual French/English booklet with 4 audio CDs of calls of 327 Indian Ocean bird species.

The Birds of Africa, vol VIII: Birds of the Malagasy Region. Roger Safford & Frank Hawkins (2013). Christopher Helm/Bloomsbury. The most comprehensive reference to the region's avifauna. Fully illustrated with plates.

Reptiles and frogs

A Field Guide to the Amphibians and Reptiles of Madagascar (3rd ed). Frank Glaw & Miguel Vences (2007). Frosch Verlag. A thoroughly updated look at the island's herpetofauna. Clearly written and illustrated with over 1,500 photos. Pricey but essential for those with a special interest in these animals. Also published in Malagasy.

A Fieldguide to the Chameleons of Madagascar. Gilles & Aurelia Moynot (2005). Aiza Edition. Trilingual French/English/Malagasy descriptions of 42 chameleons with illustrations, distribution maps and identification keys.

Chameleons Chris Mattison & Nick Garbutt (2012). Natural History Museum, London. In-depth coverage of all aspects of chameleon natural history with reference to numerous Malagasy species.

Frogs of Madagascar Genus Mantella: Pocket Identification Guide. Olga Jovanovic et al (2007). Conservation International (Tropical Pocket Guide Series). Laminated checklist with 40 photos and distribution maps for all 16 species plus 4 undescribed species.

The Tortoises and Turtles of Madagascar. Miguel Pedrono (2008). Natural History Publications. Detailed coverage of the Malagasy chelonians, living and extinct.

The Calls of the Frogs of Madagascar. Miguel Vences, Frank Glaw & Rafael Marquez (2006). Booklet and 3 audio CDs with 294 frog recordings.

Geckos of Madagascar. Patrick Schönecker (2008). Chimaira/Terralog. A lavishly illustrated hardback glossy guide to all Malagasy geckos with maps. Bilingual English/German.

Flora

Field Guide to the Orchids of Madagascar. Phillip Cribb & Johan Hermans (2009). Kew. Guide to Malagasy orchids illustrated with over 750 colour photos.

Field Guide to the Palms of Madagascar. John Dransfield et al (2006). Kew. A guide to more than a hundred of Madagascar's palms with over 180 colour photos. Ideal for field identification.

Atlas of the Vegetation of Madagascar. Justin Moat & Paul Smith (2007). Kew. Bilingual French/English atlas with 36 detailed A3 maps showing vegetation type and level of protection, and detailed text on habitats and climate.

BACKGROUND READING

100 Animals to See Before They Die. Nick Garbutt with Mike Unwin (2007). Bradt. A look at the some of the world's most threatened and unusual mammals. Includes a whole chapter on Madagascar.

Madagascar: Safari Companion. Alain Pons & Christine Baillet (2007). Evans Mitchell. A tour of the flora and fauna of Madagascar giving practical advice on photographing the wildlife. Also published in French.

Tsingy: Stone Forest – Madagascar. Olivier Grunewald & David Wolozan (2006). Editions Altus. A stunning, mainly photographic coffee-table book about Tsingy de Bemaraha. Also published in French.

Lords and Lemurs: Mad Scientists, Kings with Spears, and the Survival of Diversity in Madagascar. Alison Jolly (2004). Houghton Mifflin. A mix of lemur tales, socio-political analysis, history of Berenty reserve, and the author's experiences in Madagascar – a fascinating read.

Masoala: The Eye of the Forest. Alex Rübel et al (2003). Gut Verlag. Rainforest conservation and history of Madagascar's largest national park. Also published in French and German.

Antipode: Seasons with the Extraordinary Wildlife and Culture of Madagascar. Heather Heying (2002). St Martin's Press. The author's portrayal of life as a researcher studying green-backed mantellas in Madagascar.

The Eighth Continent: Life, Death, and Discovery in the Lost World of Madagascar. Peter Tyson (2013). Bradt Travel Guides. An absorbing travelogue following four scientists' research in Madagascar.

The Aye-aye and I. Gerald Durrell (1992). HarperCollins. Gerald Durrell recounts what turned out to be his last collecting expedition to Madagascar. Republished by House of Stratus (2003) and Summersdale (2008).

Madagascar: A World out of Time. Frans Lanting (1990) with text by Alison Jolly, John Mack & Gerald Durrell. Hale. A stunning, sometimes surreal photographic essay of the people, wildlife and landscapes of Madagascar.

Lemurs of the Lost World. Jane Wilson (1990). Impact Books. A fascinating account of the author's expeditions to the Ankarana caves in northern Madagascar.

A World Like Our Own: Man and Nature in Madagascar. Alison Jolly (1980). Tales of conservation in Madagascar, with photos by Russ Kinne.

Zoo Quest to Madagascar. David Attenborough (1961). Lutterworth. An early account of some of the first-ever filming trips to Madagascar.

DVDs

To the Island of the Aye-Aye: Gerald Durrell. Green Umbrella (2005). DVD following Durrell's quest to set up a captive breeding programme for the aye-aye. 51mins.

In the Wild: Operation Lemur with John Cleese. IMC Vision (1998). DVD in which comedian Cleese visits the captive-release programme for black-and-white ruffed lemurs at Betampona. 55mins.

Laliostoma labrosum is an explosive breeder (see page 132). (DA)

ENCOUNTER
MADAGASCAR
Get close to nature

TAILOR MADE
TRIPS

WILDLIFE
TOUR

INCENTIVE
AND GROUPS

BEACH
HOLIDAYS

ADVENTURE
TRIPS

Mail: info@encountermada.mg Skype: encounter.mada

www.encounter-mada.com
Tel: (261) 2022 31210 / Fax: (261) 2022 31222